War Admiral

THOROUGHBRED
Legends®

War Admiral

Man o' War's Greatest Son

E D W A R D   L .   B O W E N

ECLIPSE
PRESS

Guilford, Connecticut

ECLIPSE PRESS

An imprint of Globe Pequot, the trade division
of The Rowman & Littlefield Publishing Group, Inc.
4501 Forbes Blvd., Ste. 200
Lanham, MD 20706
www.rowman.com

Distributed by NATIONAL BOOK NETWORK

British Library Cataloguing in Publication Information available

Library of Congress Cataloging-in-Publication Data

Names: Bowen, Edward L., author.
Title: War Admiral : Man o' War's greatest son / Edward L. Bowen.
Description: Guilford, Connecticut : Eclipse Press, [2022] | Series:
    Thoroughbred legends | Includes bibliographical references and index.
Identifiers: LCCN 2021043009 (print) | LCCN 2021043010 (ebook) | ISBN
    9781493063208 (paperback) | ISBN 9781493064960 (epub)
Subjects: LCSH: War Admiral (Race horse) | Race horses—United States—
    Biography.
Classification: LCC SF355.W37 B69 2021 (print) | LCC SF355.W37 (ebook)
    | DDC 798.40092/9—dc23
LC record available at https://lccn.loc.gov/2021043009
LC ebook record available at https://lccn.loc.gov/2021043010

♾️™ The paper used in this publication meets the minimum requirements
of American National Standard for Information Sciences—Permanence of
Paper for Printed Library Materials, ANSI/NISO Z39.48-1992.

WAR ADMIRAL

CONTENTS

INTRODUCTION

A Paradox

War Admiral was a horse of paradoxes. He was a son of Man o' War, but initially did not suit Man o' War's owner. Physically, War Admiral had little resemblance to the heroic mold of his great bronze sire and most of his other noted sons, and yet it was he who became the best of those sons. One more paradox: He is often associated in history with his loss to Seabiscuit in the 1938 Pimlico Special, and yet many horsemen and historians have generally regarded War Admiral overall the better of the two!

There was no paradox, however, in the red badge of courage War Admiral earned and wore. Even more fundamental to his image than the race against Seabiscuit is his performance in the Belmont Stakes. It was at the start of that classic of 1937 that the little colt cut a hoof so severely that he would trail blood throughout the mile and a half around spacious Belmont Park. He would not let pain or alarm dissuade him from his appointed task, as he completed his Triple Crown in triumph.

A champion Thoroughbred, son of a Titan, in a display of class, stamina, and pure courage: No paradox there.

Edward L. Bowen
Versailles, Kentucky, 2002

CHAPTER 1

Ugly Duckling Or Crown Prince?

Collectively, the sons and daughters of Man o' War added to the exalted status of the flashy animal who had become a national hero as the decade of World War I segued into the dawn of the roaring twenties. There was about Man o' War's career at stud none of the scent of disappointment or qualified success of latter day Titans Citation and Secretariat. Man o' War led the sire list, set records, and begot fiery, classic colts and elegant, staying fillies.

Still, no one son could emerge as the equal of the sire. Fact probably supported this, but legend guaranteed it. Around Man o' War was a heroic aura that was abetted over the years by the lyric resonance of one Will Harbut. As Man o' War's groom over much of his life, Harbut took it upon himself to dramatize the facts to thousands of visitors who made the pilgrimage to

Faraway Farm to look upon the wonder horse.

The saga of Man o' War stood on its own merits, as well. He was bred by Major August Belmont II, for many years the most prominent racing man in America, breeder and owner of champions, chairman of The Jockey Club, racing commissioner — a veritable one-man legislative, judicial, and executive branch combined. Belmont's commitment to the Cape Cod Canal project diminished his business fortunes, and when World War I further complicated his personal circumstances, he decided he should sell most of his yearling crop of 1918 rather than retain the horses to race. Belmont was in his sixties but found a way to help the war effort. He took a post in Spain with the Quartermaster Corps to procure supplies for the American Expeditionary Forces.

Belmont held several fillies out of his sale, to preserve them as future broodmares, and he flirted with the idea of holding out one particular colt. This was a chestnut son of Belmont's high-class racehorse and exceptional stallion Fair Play. The colt's dam, Mahubah, was a daughter of English Triple Crown winner Rock Sand.

Belmont had been unsuccessful in peddling packages of his yearlings privately, so a draft wound up at auction at Saratoga in the summer of 1918. Man o' War did not top the sale, but at five thousand dollars was a pretty expensive purchase at the time. The winning bid was placed on behalf of Samuel D. Riddle, a sportsman of merit who had been a foxhunter, showhorse exhibitor and trainer, as well as having raced a stable of flat runners.

Riddle was a sort of Clarence Day among sportsmen. Like the Broadway character in the play *Life With Father*, Riddle was possessed of considerable self assurance, and perhaps not overly concerned with the rights or sensibilities of others. We have this via Riddle's own words, for he was quoted late in life of his decision to be nice to everyone, appending "I wasn't always." Others saw in Riddle a likeness to a Roman senator.

Harry Scott, the Kentucky horseman whose father managed Faraway Farm for the Riddle family, recalls from his own youth that the irascibility of Riddle was pivotal to the career of Man o' War's son, War Admiral. As Scott recalls with wry humor, Riddle was not impressed with the brown colt, War Admiral

being more in the runtish image of his dam, the little bay Brushup, than in the proud and masculine golden bronze of his high-headed sire.

Riddle owned Faraway with fellow sportsman and racing leader Walter M. Jeffords Sr., whose wife was the niece of Riddle's wife. While the two elements of the family held Faraway together, until Riddle eventually decreed that it should be split, the two raced separate and competing stables. There were various instances of Riddle versus Jeffords clashes, which must have created a certain tension around the dinner table. Indeed, the Jeffordses purchased Golden Broom out of the same Saratoga auction from which Riddle acquired Man o' War. Golden Broom three times beat Man o' War in schooling trials, although no match for the colt beloved as Big Red once they got into actual competition. In a more benign, cooperative form of competition, Mrs. Sarah Jeffords entered her Hoodwink against Man o' War for the 1920 Lawrence Realization so that the event was a two-horse race rather than a walkover. Man o' War made little distinction between that "race" and a walkover and won by one hundred lengths.

11

Whether Riddle were a gracious winner in such circumstance or not, we can imagine him harrumphing a bit on other occasions of family combat. In one instance, Jeffords' Edith Cavell received thirty-three pounds of actual weight from Riddle's marvelous Crusader and upset him in the 1926 Pimlico Cup. The result would have pleased Man o' War though, for he was the sire of both winner and runner-up. In 1925 the families each had a three-year-old Man o' War filly regarded as one of the two best of her age, the Jeffords filly Florence Nightingale taking the Coaching Club American Oaks, the Riddle miss Maid at Arms capturing the Alabama. Whether he took the opportunity we cannot say, but Riddle had the chance to be the gracious and sympathetic winner on the latter occasion, for Florence Nightingale finished last.

Flash forward to the mid-1930s, as Scott recalls, and we find Riddle trying to convince Jeffords to take the Man o' War—Brushup colt for his own stable.

After all, Riddle was used to the great successes of such as Crusader and American Flag, classic-winning colts cast in an heroic similarity to their sire. It seemed unlikely to Riddle that War Admiral was the stuff of classics.

Jeffords apparently felt the discomfiting evenings that would result were he to take the little colt and have him turn out successfully would not be worth it. No matter his disdain for War Admiral, Riddle would have felt true displeasure had the colt triumphed under another man's colors. Thus, for family tranquility, the younger man turned down War Admiral, consigning his irascible kinsman-by-marriage to retain a future Triple Crown winner and highly important stallion. The text of the Turf is full of such lessons that warn the successful against admiring too much their own wisdom and too little the saucy wink of lady luck.

Taking conjecture one step further, we might suspect that the anticipated wrath of Riddle was not just a small consideration, but an important one in Jeffords' declining to take the colt, for Jeffords himself had been instrumental in the acquisition of Brushup.

Part and parcel of the legend of Man o' War has been a frequent condemnation of Riddle for his failure to give the horse a maximum chance at stud, through his restrictions on allowing outside mares and the indifferent quality of his own broodmare band. While this is true to some degree, it is not altogether fair to

Riddle. Indeed, at the outset of Man o' War's career at stud, Faraway's manager at the time, Elizabeth Daingerfield, employed the assistance of English blood-stock adviser William Allison in purchasing a draft of mares abroad. Jeffords was also involved, and six mares were purchased at the Newmarket sales of 1920 and 1921, ranging in prices from $15,750 to $2,730. To have paid as much as $15,750 for a mare in the early 1920s would indicate Riddle had some understanding of the need to upgrade his mares since he now had as great a horse as Man o' War to breed to them.

At any rate, of the purchase of War Admiral's second dam, Annette K., the late Joseph Estes, then editor of *The Blood-Horse*, wrote that she was "imported *in utero* by Walter M. Jeffords and was given to Mr. Riddle." Thus, there was an added twist to the situation when Mr. Riddle was trying to turn the grandson of one gift horse into another one, while dealing with the same party!

Annette K. was a foal of 1921 and was in the last English-conceived crop of Harry of Hereford before Lord Derby sold him to France, to a syndicate represented by the Marquis de Saint Sauveur. Harry of

Hereford was a non-winner, but as a brother to the St. Leger winner Swynford, an important sire influence both here and abroad, he had been given a chance at Lord Derby's stud. Annette K.'s dam, Bathing Girl, by Spearmint, was bred by Sledmere Stud and was sold as a yearling for 610 guineas to Lord Michelham. She was unraced, as was her own dam, Summer Girl. Captain Adye of Compton Stud later purchased Bathing Girl. She had foaled a colt by Gay Lally before Captain Adye bred her to Harry of Hereford. Thus carrying Annette K., Bathing Girl was consigned to the 1920 Newmarket December sales, and for four thousand dollars became one of the mares William Allison acquired for the Riddles and Jeffordses.

There was an absence of close-up racing success in the female family of Man o' War, and this desultory pattern was to be mirrored in the female ancestry of his greatest son. Annette K., named for the famed swimmer Annette Kellerman, tread water in her only race, at two, finishing unplaced. In 1928 Annette K. was bred to Sweep, a successful stallion whose male line was of an old American dynasty (Ben Brush, Bramble, etc.) and whose broodmare sire, Domino, was the star of another

American line. Annette K.'s Sweep foal, born in 1929, was the filly Brushup. Although destined to be the dam of a Triple Crown winner, Brushup followed her immediate female ancestry in failing to win. She made three starts at two and had a second and a third.

Annette K., however, produced the nice stakes winner War Glory when bred to Man o' War. War Glory won the Walden Handicap at two in 1932, and his half sister Brushup was selected among the mares to visit the great stallion in 1933. Brushup's first foal, born that year, was by one of Man o' War's young sons, Riddle's Belmont Stakes winner American Flag. (War Glory further encouraged the cross of Man o' War and the Annette K. family when he added substantially to his record at three, winning the Lawrence Realization, Dwyer, and three other stakes.)

In *The Great Ones*, Kent Hollingsworth wrote that farm manager Harrie B. Scott "suggested the mating of Brushup and Man o' War." In addition to combining revered sire lines, the combination "matched opposites in conformation, Man o' War measuring more than six inches taller than Brushup."

The official breeding record of Brushup does not

relate how Riddle responded to his disappointment in the young colt, in terms of his plans for the mare. Brushup was bred to Man o' War again when War Admiral was but a foal, and for two years afterward she had no other reported offspring. Thus, when she was returned to Man o' War again and again later, it was with the knowledge that War Admiral was something out of the ordinary. Something very much ordinary resulted the five other times Brushup had Man o' War foals, all fillies. Nor did Brushup produce anything of note in later years to the covers of Grand Slam, Mahmoud, Blenheim II, War Relic, or Somali II.

John Hervey, writing after the fact of War Admiral's emergence in *American Race Horses of 1937*, extolled the physical loveliness of Brushup, while concurring that she was a very small Thoroughbred: "The get of Sweep were, for the most part, on the small side and, like him, without marked elegance in either form or finish.

"But Brushup is one of the most exquisite little mares imaginable...Brushup...is but 14.3 3/4 hands high, while her dam, Annette K., is but 15.0 3/4 hands.

"Her (Brushup) disposition is quiet and amiable and her manners pleasant. Her head is lovely, with a dainty muzzle and almost Arabian outline, her neck of good length and finely shaped, she is a broad-breasted little thing, with shoulders possibly a trifle straight, quarters as round and smooth as a red apple, there is little slant to her croup and her tail is set on rather high. For her size her limbs are of good bone and are admirably formed."

Armed with the hindsight of a Triple Crown, Hervey praised War Admiral for the very thing Riddle had been disquieted by, i.e., his resemblance to the dam:

"From his shoulders back, War Admiral is almost a duplicate of his dam in conformation...He is a rich brown while she is a bright bay with black points, but the son presents his mother's smooth, shapely and compact conformation, upon a slightly larger scale." (At three, War Admiral was measured at 15.2 1/4 hands.)

It was one thing to say a Triple Crown winner benefited from looking like his dam; it was another for Sam Riddle to say two years earlier that his smallish yearling colt by Man o' War looked a bit too much like his little non-winning dam, Brushup.

For some fifteen years, Riddle had reveled in his

status as Man o' War's owner. First this role found him as the master of a marvelous racehorse who won twenty of twenty-one races, earned a record $249,465, and was renowned as the most photographed and celebrated horse of all time. Then, as Man o' War's stud career had proceeded, Riddle was the owner of the public idol whose eloquent groom, Will Harbut, charmed thousands of visitors with his sonorous tales of the Thoroughbred known as "Big Red."

Now, for better or worse, Riddle was pointing yet another crop of Man o' War colts and fillies toward their debuts at the races as two-year-olds. Brushup's little man, War Admiral, was among them.

CHAPTER 2

Sportsmen Of Style And Depth

Although Faraway Farm was in Kentucky, Sam Riddle and his wife were more denizens of Pennsylvania and Maryland than of the Bluegrass. They tended to visit Faraway only a time or two a year.

Riddle was born on July 1, 1861, in Glen Riddle, a Pennsylvania village named for his father, founder of a textile plant there. Riddle was not totally averse to his family firm, but hunting and fishing were more to his taste. He married Elizabeth Dobson, whose own family's textile wealth was such that it was said when Riddle puffed up and grandly pronounced the day he bought Man o' War the greatest day of his life, she had the ready rejoinder, "Sam, the greatest day of your life was the day you married me."

The Riddles owned a six-thousand-acre farm in Pennsylvania, where they raised Hereford, Guernsey, and Ayrshire cattle, along with poultry and hogs. Riddle was president of the Rose Tree Hunt, revered as the oldest such establishment in the United States. In his marvelous historical volume, *Steeplechasing: A Complete History of the Sport in North America* (The Derrydale Press, 2000), Peter Winants places its origins in 1859. During that year Rose Tree's initial two races for members were held over cross-country courses, with hunting prints issued as the prizes. Later, the Rose Tree meetings were held over a course near Media, Pennsylvania, where its last races were staged more than a century afterward, in 1973.

The Riddles also owned an enormous property, 17,000 acres, on Maryland's Eastern Shore. At Berlin, Maryland, Riddle had a training center, named Glen Riddle, where trainer Louis Feustel had primed Man o' War for his debut at two and then honed him again for his return at three in 1920. In the winter of 1935-36, another trainer, George Conway, had a similar task with War Admiral and his fellow Riddle-bred youngsters.

An appealing aspect of this Man o' War-War Admiral tale is the lengthy involvement of certain individuals. Riddle, of course, was owner of one and breeder-owner of another. Feustel, who trained Man o' War throughout the colt's racing days, had a longer connection to the background of Big Red, having been confronted as a youngster with the task of riding Man o' War's dangerously irascible grandsire, Hastings. Feustel later had been foreman when Andrew Jackson Joyner trained Hastings' son and Man o' War's sire, the crack Fair Play, for August Belmont II. Moreover, Feustel had been given a division of the Belmont stable in time to train Mahubah, destined to be the dam of Man o' War.

When Feustel trained Man o' War, his foreman was George Conway. On a number of occasions, Conway's duties included accompanying the highly strung Man o' War to the post. Now, in 1936, Conway had had a decade's worth of experience as Riddle's trainer, and he was supervising War Admiral's early tutoring at Berlin.

Conway, like Feustel before him, had trod the path of preparedness through years of toil that typified the top trainers of his day. A youngster setting out as an underling at a racing stable was not likely to be a lad with a great many options, so he was content — or had to be content — with a long apprenticeship of mucking stalls, walking hots, and grooming.

Among the various tellings of Conway's early life is at least one account that would have us believe he was galloping horses at age eight or nine! His age became an issue in one of the few jocular comments ever attributed to him. In *The Morning Telegraph* article of 1937, Conway, by then recognized as the trainer of Derby-Preakness winner War Admiral, quipped, "I certainly did not have anything to do with Proctor Knott when he won the first Futurity. I'm not THAT old!"

The gag was that a few sentences later the article revealed Conway did, in fact, have a recollection of Proctor Knott's defeat of Salvator in the 1888 Futurity, but that he was "only a kid" at the time.

Conway was born in Oceanport, New Jersey. His obituary in 1939 in *The New York Times*, with a dateline of that town, placed his age at sixty, which would have indicated he was born about 1879. Various other articles, however, mentioned his reticence about revealing his age and estimated him to be "about 70" at the time of his death. This would mean he was nearing twenty when Proctor Knott was two and might well have had more to do with the horse than he admitted.

Either birth date would have meant that his entrance

onto the racing scene could have been abetted by the emergence of nearby Monmouth Park as one of the swank racecourses of the latter decades of the nineteenth century.

According to *The Morning Telegraph*, Conway caught on with the similarly opulent Rancocas Stable, the headquarters from which Pierre Lorillard had sent out a brigade of runners, the dominance of which approached that of Calumet Farm of a later era. Conway often was described as having been a protégé of Matt Byrnes. In 1886 Byrnes left Rancocas — because Lorillard retired from racing that year — and continued his career as trainer for James Ben Ali Haggin. In another version of Conway's tale, a man identified as "Maj. Tom McCreery's father" was said to be the young man's boss at Rancocas, where presumably there were a number of horses maintained even after Lorillard had quit the Turf. Conway also worked later for another Jersey outfit, the Eaton Stud of Andrew Albright.

In a 1937 interview *The Morning Telegraph* commented, "It is a great advantage for a lad starting out with horses to find himself with good horses. Good horses are usually cared for by smart horsemen who can teach a youngster everything that he is capable of learning. That George Conway learned all his mentors could teach him he proved in later years, first as foreman for Samuel Riddle and then as trainer for the man who until this year was best known as Man o' War's owner.

"The first good horse Conway was connected with was a mare named Blush, who won valuable stakes many years ago, but he will always be associated with Man o' War in the public mind. Big Red was Conway's special charge when he was burning up the track. When Man o' War came along the veteran had been foreman of the Riddle stable for several years. It was he who led the champion to the post."

An article published in *The Blood-Horse* in 1937, at the height of Conway's fame, attributed some details from the most knowledgeable possible source, Conway himself:

"Quiet and undemonstrative George Conway was finally waylaid and persuaded to tell the palpitating public some facts relative to the charges he has trained over the past 30-odd years.

"By his own admission, the first winner he ever trained was the brown filly Evening... bred by Andrew

Albright at his Eaton Stud, Eatontown, N. J., and raced in the name and colors of H. J. Morris.

"The date was June 8, 1905, the place Gravesend...

"As to the best race horse he ever saw, George Conway is inclined to award the palm to Man o' War. But when it comes to the question as to the best filly he ever saw, he finds it difficult to decide among Miss Woodford, Firenze, and Dewdrop — he still retains a great respect for the (last-named) daughter of Falsetto out of Explosion, bred in New Jersey by Pierre Lorillard as long ago as 1883. For as Mr. Conway pointed out, 'you have got to think a great deal of a mare you saw win the Great Eastern, the Nursery, and Champagne at two, beating such as Inspector B., and then as a 3-year-old dead-heating with The Bard in the Spindrift, win the Monmouth Oaks, the Stockton, Stevens, Palisades, Eatontown, West End, and First Special Stakes. Who knows how much farther she might have gone..." Dewdrop died on September 11, 1886, as a three-year-old.

Thus, by his own comments, Conway identified himself as quite knowledgeable with champion horses of the middle 1880s. It is possible, of course, but unlikely, that he would have been seven or eight at

the time, which would be the case were the published 1879 birth date accurate.

Press reports of the late 1930s also note that when Eaton Stud was dispersed after the death of its owner, Conway set out on his own, campaigning a few horses for himself and some for Harry Morris, a gentleman rider of steeplechase horses. Conway was reported to have been given a division of Samuel Riddle's horses as early as 1914, although his post was as foreman several years later.

When Feustel left the Riddle stable, he was succeeded as head trainer by Gwyn Tompkins. Conway stayed on, and when Tompkins retired at the beginning of 1926, Riddle turned to his loyal employee as his next head trainer. Life would permit Conway little more than a dozen more years. Professionally, he might be said to have made the most of them.

It was early in the days of Man o' War's sons and daughters at the races, and Tompkins had used some of them to go out with a very good year. In 1925 American Flag was a star three-year-old by Man o' War. (Man o' War had been named by Mrs. August Belmont II, who observed the prevailing world circumstance of 1918 by giving the entire crop military names. Riddle frequently followed that pattern with the horse's offspring. Hence, American Flag, Crusader, War Admiral, etc.)

Under Tompkins' tutelage in his last year as head trainer, American Flag added to the burgeoning glory of Man o' War as a stallion when he carried the yellow-and-black Riddle colors to victories in three of the most important races in New York: the Belmont Stakes, Withers Stakes, and Dwyer. There was no official championship voting at the time, but racing historians traditionally regard American Flag as the best three-year-old colt of 1925. Another Riddle homebred, Maid at Arms, is reckoned to have been co-champion three-year-old filly of that year. Late in the 1925 racing season, Tompkins had a particularly gratifying hour when on October 24 at Laurel he sent out the two-year-old Crusader to win the $10,000 Manor Handicap and followed up with Maid at Arms' victory in the $10,000 Maryland Handicap in the next race. He surely left Conway a high standard to maintain.

American Flag failed to win any additional stakes at four in Conway's first year as head trainer. Any criticism that might have come the way of the soft-spoken horse-

man was assuaged, however, by his guidance of another Man o' War colt to prominence. This was Crusader, often said to have resembled the sire's fire and handsomeness more than any other son. Crusader emerged in time to defeat his older stablemate, American Flag, as they ran one-two in the Suburban Handicap. He also won the Belmont Stakes and Jockey Club Gold Cup among an impressive year's total of nine major stakes victories in the East and Midwest. Historians regarded him as the champion three-year-old of 1926.

The following year Conway brought him back at four. Crusader won but one additional stakes, but that was a repeat in the Suburban. The Suburban Handicap had burst onto the American racing scene as a highly important race from its inaugural in 1884, and it had been a major target of many champions in the ensuing forty-plus years, but no horse had contrived to win it twice, until Crusader.

Between Crusader's era and War Admiral's, the Riddle stable and Conway did not have extraordinary success, despite the prowess of Man o' War as a sire. In addition to the aforementioned War Glory, Conway won the Adirondack and Test stakes at Saratoga with

Speed Boat and the Travers Stakes, Saratoga Cup, and Huron Handicap with War Hero, both by Man o' War. Those were fine moments, centered on the fashion of Saratoga, but not a great decade for an owner who had once supped with the gods of the Turf.

It would take even War Admiral some time before Conway would place him above Crusader as the best horse he had trained. Insofar as identifying the best filly he trained, Conway gave that distinction to Argosie. A daughter of Man o' War, Argosie was a full sister to American Flag. Her designation as the trainer's best reflects the ability of racing professionals to be smitten by something other than the cold facts of the record. Argosie never won a major race. She was unsound and difficult to train, but she rallied from sixth to get within a length of the great Top Flight in the 1932 Coaching Club American Oaks. She was runner-up that day, but secured her place in the heart of her admiring trainer.

The 1937 *The Morning Telegraph* article indicated that Conway was a perfect match for Riddle, who brought to his prominence as a racing man a certain bombast and willingness to speak at length about his horses and himself.

"George Conway has no use for publicity, preferring to go about his business and let the results speak for themselves," recorded the *Telegraph*. "They are speaking particularly loud just now, thanks to the deeds of War Admiral. The Glen Riddle trainer is a shrewd student of horses, treating each one of his charges as an individual. He has no hard and fast rules, preferring to regard each horse as a separate problem in diet, work and racing tactics. Like Jim Fitzsimmons he believes in patience, patience and then more patience. His horses rarely race a great deal at two years, but when they do go to the post they are as fit as man can make them. If they can't run after that it's because they haven't got any run in them."

The comparison to Fitzsimmons was particularly apt at the moment, since the two were the only trainers of Triple Crown winners during the 1930s.

CHAPTER 3

A Promising, Subtle Start

Man o' War was nineteen when War Admiral was a two-year-old, and the progenitor lived to the age of thirty. At the time Conway took over the training of War Admiral, Man o' War had reigned as an important sire for a dozen years, but his statistics had dwindled over time. In his first five crops, Man o' War got an amazing twenty-eight percent stakes winners, twenty-six of his ninety-two foals gaining that status. In his next five crops, he got almost an identical number of additional foals, ninety-one, but only thirteen were stakes winners.

In 1936 War Admiral, however, was part of a trilogy of juveniles that might be said to have suggested a revival of Man o' War's ability to turn out multiple stars in a given crop. The Sagamore Press' wonderful series of annual books on the best horses of the year debuted at the conclusion of 1936. As was true of subsequent volumes, *American Race Horses of 1936* generally employed the format of one chapter per horse. Several exceptions were made that year by author John Hervey, who grouped horses of common ownership or other similarities. One such example was the chapter entitled "The Man o' War Flotilla," which detailed the campaigns of two sons and a daughter of the great stallion, to wit, Matey, War Admiral, and Wand. All three were two-year-olds, and their concurrent arrival at incipient stardom savored of earlier crops of Man o' War.

Hervey concluded the chapter with the carefully hedged testimony that, "So far as we are aware they present a novel instance of three different two-year-olds, all by one sire, that have won three different stakes each worth over $10,000 during the closing weeks of a season."

All three were Faraway products, but it was the Jeffordses who had the stronger hand, being the breeders and (separate) owners of Matey and Wand. Jeffords might well have spent part of that autumn congratulating himself on his decision not to accept War Admiral. If he were sensitive to how his wife's old uncle might have behaved if the castoff had succeeded individually, imagine the upshot of the Jeffordses having three stars to the older fellow's none!

Matey came along late in the year to win the Pimlico Futurity, which at $15,000 not only was a very rich race for the time but as a middle-distance test for juveniles in the autumn was seen as an indicator of classic potential for the following year. (Matey's victory was a bit messy, for he got the nod in the stewards' stand, where it was decided that Eddie Arcaro, aboard the apparent winner in Calumet Farm's Privileged, was waving his hand in front of Matey's face at the finish. The officials clearly felt the gesture, and accompanying perceived bump, were something apart from a friendly "Hey, Matey!") Wand, a filly, won three of four races, culminating with the Matron Stakes, a traditional test of young distaffers in the New York autumn. War Admiral won three of six races, his acceptance into Hervey's elite company being through victory in the $10,000 Eastern Shore Stakes.

Conway found the young War Admiral far enough advanced in his training at Berlin that the trainer took him to the nearby Havre de Grace racetrack for his debut as early as April 25. Thus, at a now defunct

track still revered in older Maryland horsemen's memories, War Admiral raced his first public furlongs. He was sent off at 7.5-1 in a field of ten striplings. With jockey "Moose" Peters aboard, the lovely little colt scooted right up with the leaders from the beginning of the four and a half-furlong maiden event. It was a debut showing fighting spirit as well as quickness, for he was in a hard drive to win by a nose from Alfred Vanderbilt's Sonny Joe. Each carried 114 pounds.

Almost a month later War Admiral appeared under colors again. By this time, Conway had shipped the Riddle runners to Belmont Park, then as now the headquarters of the upscale New York circuit. Jackie Westrope was aboard War Admiral on May 21, when he took on seven others. The New Yorkers were not impressed by the Maryland form and sent him off at 10-1, a price vigorously capitalized upon by the colt's connections. Again showing early zip, he set off down the Widener Course, which used to cross diagonally across the roomy Belmont oval.

He won by two lengths in :58 4/5 for five furlongs. He carried 113 pounds, the same as runner-up Scintillator.

Scintillator flattered the form by winning the Juvenile Stakes soon after War Admiral had beaten him, and the Glen Riddle colt was given his own first chance at stakes company in the National Stallion Stakes on June 6. He was 3-1 as a close second choice in a field of ten to another unbeaten youngster, Pompoon. It was to be the first meeting with a rival he would see again the following spring. At the budding stage of their respective careers, Pompoon was the further advanced, and he outraced the field, winning by nearly two lengths. For the first time War Admiral was not with the leaders from the beginning. He was fifth at the first call and closed to be third, beaten two and a half lengths. Pompoon won in :59, one-fifth of a second slower than War Admiral's time in the earlier race down the Widener Course. Fencing finished second. War Admiral gained only about one length on the pace in the final stages of the race, although the chart noted he "moved up gamely." The top three, and most of the others in the field, each carried 122 pounds.

In Pompoon, owner J.H. Louchheim had the future champion of the division. The son of Pompey went on to win the Junior Champion and Futurity stakes. (He

also won a race with the unusual condition of all starters being owned by ladies, Mrs. Louchheim being the
listed owner of record for an overnight race named the
Diana Handicap.)

After his gallant victory in the Futurity, in which
he burst through traffic with a show of determination,
Pompoon briefly was recipient of the often employed
encomium "greatest two-year-old since..." Most horsemen of that day would have ended the sentence with
"Man o' War," although Hervey noted that there were
still some around who might have harked back farther
to Tremont, Colin, or Domino!

In the spring, however, while Pompoon had clearly
stepped up as the division leader, there had been no
such aura around him. War Admiral had seemed in the
thick of the fight for early prestige among juveniles,
but he followed his National Stallion Stakes defeat with
another, losing caste rather quickly. The second loss
came about three weeks later. Racing six furlongs, this
time around a turn at Aqueduct, War Admiral lined up
for the Great American Stakes. He was running six furlongs for the first time and, carrying 115 pounds, was
the 2-1 second choice to the gelding Fairy Hill (113).

Charley Kurtsinger was aboard the Riddle colt for the first time, and he set him on the lead early. Always under pressure, War Admiral continued in front deep into the stretch, but Fairy Hill closed so quickly that he raced off to a one and one-half-length victory in 1:12 3/5. The chart noted that War Admiral "weakened."

The form of the Great American was later to receive a boost when Maedic, whom War Admiral had beaten two lengths for second, put on an amazing winning skein at Saratoga. A colt that had already made six starts in Florida before the end of February, Maedic continued in high activity in the following months. He reached Saratoga with sixteen races behind him, and the pace quickened. He swept no fewer than five juvenile stakes at the Spa meeting, accounting for the Flash, Saratoga Sales, Sanford, Grand Union Hotel, and Hopeful stakes. The reputation Maedic thus engendered was diminished somewhat by the fact that the racetrack cough swept through and put a number of juveniles out of action for the Saratoga meeting.

To have outfinished Maedic did not put much of a shine on War Admiral's second loss at the time, however, and the Riddle colt suffered an understandable loss in

public esteem. The stable continued to have confidence in him, but there were to be many weeks before Conway could give him a chance to redeem himself. War Admiral was among the Eastern two-year-olds hit by the coughing epizootic that summer. He had to be withdrawn from all action at Saratoga, where the Riddles were famous for entertaining friends with mint juleps and accessories at their handsome house near the racecourse.

Whether the incipient effects of the cough had anything to do with War Admiral's effort in the Great American we cannot tell, but he did not appear under colors again for two and a half months. Given Conway's approach, the horseman might have been privately glad of the need to stop and let War Admiral have a break. War Admiral had not been nominated to any of the key futurities of the day, the Belmont Futurity, Pimlico Futurity, and New England Futurity, a decision harking back to Riddle's early dislike of him.

Since War Admiral was not eligible for the richest, the Belmont Futurity to be run on October 3, Conway had him back in Maryland by the time he next raced. That he would go directly into a $10,000 race without a prep after such a layoff underscores Conway's confidence in the colt. The Eastern Shore Handicap of six furlongs was run on September 19 at the old Havre de Grace track, and it attracted a field of fifteen. The topweight at 126 pounds and the favorite at 18-10 was Maedic, still racing unrelentingly. Bottle Cap, who like Maedic was a son of Bostonian, had won or placed in eight of his nine races and was second choice in the Eastern Shore under 120 pounds. Tedious carried 119, and War Admiral was among those weighted at 118. The Riddle colt was sent off at almost 8-1 as the third choice.

Kurtsinger was again aboard, and perhaps worried about having been drawn on the far outside, in stall fifteen, he sent War Admiral blazing from the outset. Despite the quality of the field, War Admiral dominated. He dashed a quarter-mile in :22 3/5 and a half-mile in :45 4/5. A promise that would grow into greatness was thus being shown to the public for the first time and, if the crowd were enthralled, the other horses were stunned. War Admiral was in front by four lengths by that time, and he added another length to his margin, despite not being ridden out. He scored by five lengths over Orientalist (116), with Rex Flag (115) third, and Bottle Cap and Maedic fourth and fifth,

respectively. The final time of 1:11 was only two-fifths over the track record.

"The race was truly run and brilliantly won and served to lift the winner high in public and expert estimation," Hervey wrote. It also had the effect of inducing top weight for War Admiral when he next raced, in the six-furlong Richard Johnson Handicap at another Maryland track, Laurel, on October 10. War Admiral was assigned 124 pounds, while Bottle Cap got in at 119, a swing of seven pounds. The second highweight at 120 was Billionaire, a full brother to Kentucky Derby winner Brokers Tip. Billionaire won the Wakefield Handicap and placed later in the Pimlico Futurity.

The track was muddy and testing, but Kurtsinger again put War Admiral right out on top. The colt fought hard but could not keep the lead at the weight spread, and Bottle Cap drew away to defeat him by one and one-half lengths in 1:12 3/5.

It was an anticlimactic follow up of his brilliant Eastern Shore. Similarly, the Futurity winner Pompoon was beaten by Reaping Reward when he was sent out to try to add the New England Futurity as a closing statement for the year.

Daily Racing Form began its annual balloting for champions in 1936, and Pompoon won in the two-year-old colt division. He was, moreover, widely perceived as the winter favorite for the Kentucky Derby. He had won six of eight races and earned $82,260. At year's end, however, Pompoon was assigned only second-highest impost of 125 pounds on the Experimental Free Handicap. In compiling that handicap, John B. Campbell must have gotten caught up in trying to plumb potential rather than assessing the racing season just passed. He placed top weight of 126 on Colonel E. R. Bradley's Blue Larkspur colt, Brooklyn, whose sole stakes victory came in the Walden Handicap. Brooklyn was moved to second in the Pimlico Futurity when Privileged was disqualified. Brooklyn had been in the headlines a year earlier when, as a yearling, he was bid in for his breeder, Bradley, at $20,000 at Saratoga. It was reported that a live bid of $19,500 represented Ethel V. Mars, of the leading Milky Way Stable, but that she did not hear the next attempt to gouge her further and did not realize there was a bid against her until it was too late.

In addition to the esteem shown for Brooklyn, at

least some observers, including Neil Newman, review-ing 1936 for the *Bloodstock Breeders' Review* of England, regarded Reaping Reward as the most promising colt for the three-year-old classics. The latter publication made no mention of War Admiral in its review of the division, although *The Blood-Horse*'s Golden Anniversary edition, covering 1916-1940, retrospectively included him in its rating for juveniles that year as follows: Pompoon, Reaping Reward, Arlington Futurity winner Case Ace, Privileged, War Admiral, Maedic, etc. (There was no mention of Brooklyn in the latter assessment.)

War Admiral was assigned 121 on the Experimental, below six others. He had won three of six races, with two seconds and a third, and earned $14,800.

After his final race, War Admiral had but a short trip back to winter quarters at Berlin, Maryland. Man o' War, American Flag, Crusader, etc., had also spent months of growth and power building at Glen Riddle between their juvenile and classic-age seasons. Now, once again, a masterful horseman had at hand the raw material to guide into greatness. It would not be an opportunity missed.

CHAPTER 4

Crown Upon A Noble Brow

F ew facts in the history of racing are repeated more than that the most famous of horses, Man o' War, "never" won the most famous of races, the Kentucky Derby. When expressed with irony, "never" indicates a failure on the general public's part to recognize that the Derby is for three-year-olds, so no horse has more than one chance at it. Be that as it may, it was Samuel D. Riddle's perception that running one and one-quarter miles in early May was too much to ask of a three-year-old. It has also been alleged that Riddle did not care much for Kentucky racing. Indeed, *The Blood-Horse* report of the 1937 Kentucky Derby carried the comment that "Mr. Riddle shunned Kentucky racing, confined his stable almost entirely to Maryland and New York, despite the fact that many of his horses appeared excellent Kentucky Derby prospects." The fact that, as long ago as 1926, Riddle had allowed Crusader to be sent to what was then called "the West" to win the Cincinnati Derby at Latonia perhaps tempers the broad-stroke belief he disapproved of that circuit.

At any rate, it was made clear at the start of the season that Riddle was allowing a trainer to think in terms of the Kentucky Derby, and War Admiral would be his first nominee. One can conjecture that the importance of the Triple Crown had something to do with this change in policy. In Man o' War's time, the Kentucky Derby, Preakness, and Belmont Stakes were not recognized as the American Triple Crown. Sir Barton had won all three races the year before and certainly was acclaimed for that achievement, but the three races were not officially linked. In 1930 Gallant Fox became the second horse to sweep the three races.

Many years later, when Secretariat was enthralling the world by ending a drought of Triple Crown winners, it was widely accepted that Charlie Hatton had coined the phrase "Triple Crown" as applied to the Derby, Preakness, and Belmont. Hatton, himself, was still authoring lovely prose for *Daily Racing Form* at the time, and he pushed the concept of his own prescience in print so often that it took on the clout of accepted dogma. More than one source, however, carries the version that Bryan Field, a writer who later was manager of Delaware Park and an ardent television racing commentator, first applied the phrase to the races in question in 1930.

Hatton was writing for *The Blood-Horse*, under the name Old Rosebud, in 1930, when Gallant Fox won the Derby, Preakness, and Belmont. The magazine's report of the Belmont contained the comment that "the two (Sir Barton and Gallant Fox) might be called Triple Event winners." Although the specific article was unsigned, we cannot resist speculating that based upon this sentence Hatton developed the bravery to equate the series with its English origin and later staked his claim for having codified the linking of the three. The term "Triple Crown" had previously been applied in England to the Two Thousand Guineas, Epsom Derby, and St. Leger. The phrase's English origins also seem to have been vague. In 1935, when Bahram swept those three races, the reporter in the *Bloodstock Breeders' Review* contented himself with the comment that the colt had swept "what has long been called the Triple

Crown." (In this country, Gallant Fox's son, Omaha, had in the same year added a third name to the winners of our version of the Triple.)

As Man o' War developed between racing seasons, a full eight months passed between his final race at two and his debut at three. In War Admiral's case, the span was not quite so pronounced. Still, six months passed between the end of one campaign and the launch of another. This might surprise observers, considering today's presumption that the shorter gap between the Breeders' Cup Classic and, say, the Florida Derby (four months) will be interrupted by at least one prep race.

The Havre de Grace meeting began April 12. War Admiral had been sent there some time before and quickly became the talk of the backstretch. Two days into the meeting, George Conway presented his protégé in public for an allowance race. Once again, he was assaying a trip of six furlongs. The local colt was sent off at odds of slightly less than 4-5, although a couple of colts, Airflame (117 pounds) and Clingendaal (111), were known to be speedsters. Conditions called for War Admiral to carry top weight of 120 pounds.

Charley Kurtsinger was again aboard War Admiral,

and he again shot the colt into an early lead. Airflame thought himself a challenge, but he was turned back confidently. War Admiral then kept Clingendaal at bay, winning by two and one-half lengths. The fractions were :23 and :46 1/5, and the final time was 1:11 2/5. Conway and Kurtsinger knew that taller cotton awaited, and Kurtsinger persevered with War Admiral, sending him another two furlongs, for a mile clocking in 1:41. After all, the next target, the Chesapeake Stakes, was but ten days away, and then it would be only two more weeks until the Kentucky Derby, should the little colt qualify.

The decision to put the extra work into the colt was highly beneficial, for the days between the allowance race and the Chesapeake were marked by rain and heavy racetracks. Conway had the luxury of avoiding any serious work under those conditions and still apparently having sufficient confidence that he was sending a fit horse out for the $10,000 Chesapeake Stakes. At a mile and one-sixteenth, the Chesapeake was considerably longer than any of War Admiral's earlier races.

His old rival Fairy Hill had been working very well. Nevertheless, War Admiral, coupled with a stablemate

named Over the Top, was sent off at slightly more than 3-5. War Admiral would become known for his altercations at the start, and on more than one occasion the official in charge of proceedings consigned him to start from outside the gates. The Chesapeake gave a preview of such behavior, and the Riddle colt was assessed a goodly share of the blame for delaying the start for seven minutes. Despite that waste of energy, coupled with the longest distance he had yet faced, War Admiral dashed right to the front and made the race his own from the beginning.

It was a "one horse race" in the words of John Hervey, as War Admiral clicked off fractions of :23 2/5, :47 2/5, 1:11 3/5, and 1:37 3/5. He dashed on to the finish in 1:45, defeating Court Scandal by six lengths, pulling up. Court Scandal had won the $20,000 Flamingo Stakes in Florida. Winner and runner-up each carried 119 pounds. Over the Top was third under 114. "Won easily" was the highly satisfactory chart conclusion of War Admiral's performance.

The facile victory in what in those days was respected as a major Derby prep thrust War Admiral to the forefront of a crop whose leaders earlier had been reck-

oned some way ahead of him. Pompoon, the champion at two, was undergoing a pre-classic regimen that
seemed designed to cast aspersions on his legitimacy
as a Derby colt, while Brooklyn had failed to train
satisfactorily. (Colonel Bradley, owner of Brooklyn, in
one of the grandiose wagers for which he was rightly
renowned, had struck a deal with Pompoon's owner.
Bradley wagered $10,000 to the other man's $11,000
that Brooklyn would finish in front of Pompoon in the
Derby.)

Pompoon came out first in a six-furlong race, the
Paumonok, which was a bit of an oddity in that it
required the three-year-old to take on a field of serious
older sprinters in his debut for the year, on April 15.
This test he passed admirably, although it was noted
that no winner of the event had won the Kentucky
Derby aside from Zev in 1923. Giving weight by scale
to the field of older horses, Pompoon won by a neck
from Tintagel in a duel of Futurity winners, while such
other accomplished campaigners as Speed to Spare and
Snark were also beaten.

An element that Hervey described alliteratively as
"the most perspicuous pundits" nonetheless took this

performance as justification for vaulting War Admiral to the top of their cogitation for the Derby. A week before the Churchill Downs race, Pompoon played into this scenario by failing to place in Melodist's Wood Memorial, then run at one mile and seventy yards.

War Admiral arrived in Louisville on April 26. As an illustration of the training philosophy of the day, he "breezed" six furlongs in 1:20 2/5 on April 30 and nine furlongs in 1:55 1/5 on May 2. On May 4, two days after one work and four days before the Derby itself, he was trained the entire mile and one-quarter distance of the Run for the Roses itself. This he accomplished in 2:08 3/5 in the rain. The verve demonstrated in that last move sent his odds dropping in relation to those offered on Reaping Reward, who had emerged as the second choice.

Just as a topper, War Admiral returned to the track to work a half-mile in :50 3/5 on the day before the Derby!

Of the War Admiral team, jockey Charley Kurtsinger was the one with Kentucky Derby experience. He had won the race six years earlier on Twenty Grand. At the time he was contract rider for the Greentree Stable of Mrs. Payne Whitney, one of the top stables in the East. Moreover, going to Churchill Downs was a homecoming for Kurtsinger, who was born in nearby Shepherdsville, Kentucky, in 1907, and first worked for the jockey-turned-trainer Roscoe Goose. Goose secured a place in Kentucky Derby lore when he rode Donerail to victory in the 1913 running. At 91-1, Donerail remains the longest-priced winner of the race.

Kurtsinger first began riding races in 1924 and had no more than nineteen wins in any season until riding sixty-four winners in 1929. He picked up nicknames along the way. Some of his fellow riders came to call him "Chicken," not in disparagement but in jealous recognition that here was one jockey not concerned with dieting and with a hearty taste for poultry. He was also often referred to as "the Flying Dutchman," or "the Little Flying Dutchman."

The phrase "the Flying Dutchman" is said to date from a 1641 incident in which a Dutch ship skippered by a Captain van der Decken ran into a storm and sank off the Cape of Good Hope. Legends grew that, over the years, other sailors, including the young King George V during his naval days, saw an image of the phantom ship in the glowing distance.

The nickname has been affixed freely since then.

The sportswriter Bill Corum, who became keeper of the flame of Derby lore as the president of Churchill Downs, wrote after Kurtsinger's death in 1946: "The big Flying Dutchman of sports was Honus Wagner (baseball)...The little Flying Dutchman was jockey Charley Kurtsinger."

A rather tall tale of how Kurtsinger got the nickname was passed along, for the public's acceptance or bemusement, by Bryan Field in a *New York Times* column of 1931. It had nothing to do with the rider's ethnic heritage, or phantom ships off the Cape of Good Hope.

"It is natural for a horseman to worry over a horse, and while there never was any need for Kurtsinger to worry about Twenty Grand...it seems that the old stallion Little Dutch was quite a different kind of horse. 'Well, you see, he had a shoulder that was dislocated and he used to carry it all out of kilter. And then he got hurt in one of his legs so that he would hobble about...,' related Kurtsinger.

"Yet it was the same Little Dutch with blond Charley on his back that won a quarter-mile race at the Bullitt County Fair."

Kurtsinger's father had been a rider, although not

a big name one, and he had impressed upon the son the principle of always riding to win. The youngster carried this to extreme once on a horse named Captain Hal in Kentucky. Kurtsinger was being crowded and retaliated with his whip, and was duly set down by the stewards. Kurtsinger was temporarily plying more humble work, with hoe and rake, when he had the colossal break of being contacted by a crack rider. Mack Garner had noted Kurtsinger's strong ability to finish and sought him out to see if he wanted to try out with the stable of William Ziegler, for whom the established jockey was riding first string. Kurtsinger won on his first mount for Ziegler, at 20-1, and quickly caught on as the number two rider for the outfit.

Garner later provided an even larger break, but not of his own intention. Ziegler had a horse named Ilium, for which he had paid $26,500 as a yearling. Garner was on that particular colt in a race in which Kurtsinger was riding a supposed inferior stablemate, Phantom Star (not Ship). Twenty Grand was also in the race, the second of his career, and was odds-on off his maiden win. Ilium had not done much to justify his high price tag to that date, and he was failing

again. Kurtsinger recognized that it was up to him, and he brought Phantom Star up to defeat Twenty Grand. Garner expressed the opinion that Ilium was "not so much horse," which generated such bad feelings within the stable that Garner wound up resigning. Suddenly Kurtsinger was the number one rider.

Later, Kurtsinger signed on with Greentree and wound up the partner, not the rival, of Twenty Grand. He rode Twenty Grand in his famous duels with Equipoise that same autumn of 1930. In the Kentucky Jockey Club Stakes at Churchill Down, Kurtsinger and Twenty Grand prevailed by a nose, although Equipoise gained his revenge later in an equally enthralling Pimlico Futurity. The following year Twenty Grand won the Wood Memorial prior to taking the Derby, and he later added the Belmont Stakes, Dwyer, Lawrence Realization, and Jockey Club Gold Cup with Kurtsinger aboard. The jockey won ninety-three races that year and led all riders in earnings with $392,095. Kurtsinger's response to such a banner year was to buy a 250-acre farm near Louisville. He also had developed the practice of donating any purse earnings he received during Colonel E. R. Bradley's charity race meeting to

the orphans' association that was also Bradley's benefi-
ciary from the day. The event was held at Bradley's Idle
Hour Farm outside Lexington.

After that big year Kurtsinger was injured, and his
win total dropped to thirty-four in 1932. Late that year,
Greentree sold his contract to Allan Ryan, owner of Anall
Stable. The rider continued to have some leaner years,
statistically, although he retained sufficient prestige to
get some major mounts from Sunny Jim Fitzsimmons
on Wheatley Stable horses. In 1934 Kurtsinger won the
Manhattan Handicap, Saratoga Cup, and Jockey Club
Gold Cup on Wheatley's Dark Secret. Tragedy tainted
the final victory, however, for Dark Secret fractured a
leg in the stretch. He courageously fought on to hold off
Faireno, but by the end of the race the leg was so dam-
aged that he could not be saved.

Kurtsinger's later affiliations included a period riding first call for Brookmeade Stable, another of the top
Eastern outfits. (As a footnote to his career, Kurtsinger
had two rides in 1934 aboard Belair Stud's Omaha
for Fitzsimmons. Omaha won neither. The following
year, though, the late-developing juvenile won the
Triple Crown with jockey Smokey Saunders aboard.

Thus, after War Admiral's Triple Crown in 1937, Kurtsinger could say he had ridden two winners of the Crown. The only rider actually to ride two Triple Crown winners was Eddie Arcaro, who won aboard Whirlaway and Citation; Arcaro also rode a third Triple Crown winner, Assault, although in other races. John Longden won the Triple Crown aboard Count Fleet and also had some mounts on Whirlaway. Riders who never won the Triple Crown but who had mounts on more than one Triple Crown winner at some point in their careers were Jimmy Stout [Omaha and Assault], Jackie Westrope [War Admiral and Whirlaway], and Angel Cordero [Seattle Slew and Affirmed]).

In 1935 Kurtsinger's win figure increased to seventy-one races. That year, he was prominent on the West Coast, where he won the Bay Meadows Handicap, San Antonio Handicap, and San Juan Capistrano on Mrs. Silas Mason's Head Play. Back East he rode the same horse to victory in the prestigious Suburban Handicap. (Kurtsinger had not been on Head Play in the famed "Fighting Finish" against Brokers Tip in the 1933 Kentucky Derby.)

So, Charley Kurtsinger was a veteran rider on

familiar territory on the spring day in 1937 when War Admiral led the elongated parade of twenty horses to the post for the Kentucky Derby. The race was still growing in national acclaim, and the crowd estimated at 75,000 was extolled as the greatest in the event's history. Betting on the single event exceeded $500,000. Among the throng was John Nance Garner, vice president of the United States. Not among it was Sam Riddle, whose physician had convinced the ailing owner to stay home in Pennsylvania.

War Admiral's being drawn on the rail was not a bargain. Even though the gate had been moved forward forty feet from its placement of earlier years — as the logistics of the then-new starting gates were worked through — it was still just enough on the turn that the inside horses risked being jammed at the start. War Admiral was favored at 3-2, with Reaping Reward heading the second-choice Milky Way Farm entry at 9-2. Pompoon, though third choice, was off at 8-1, signifying his diminished standing.

War Admiral was among several horses that were fractious, and the start was delayed for eight minutes. Thoughts of the previous year, when Granville had dumped his rider at the start, might well have set George Conway to chewing his lower lip. Nevertheless, while a rascal moments before, War Admiral was a pure professional the instant official action commenced. He darted away with alacrity and in a few strides had headed the even quicker starting Heelfly. Kurtsinger rode cautiously, taking War Admiral out a couple of paths from the rail, even though it meant some horse might benefit from saving ground. There would be little to be concerned about in this Derby, however.

War Admiral spent ten furlongs demonstrating his superiority, in the early going, all along the backstretch, through the turn, and in the testing final two furlongs. He led by a length or so for much of the way, clicking off fractions of :23 1/5, :46 4/5, 1:12 2/5. Then, when, the phrase "the real running starts" came into play, it was the frontrunner pulling away to a longer margin rather than a challenge coming from out of the pack. Heelfly had been in respectful pursuit early and then Pompoon had come along to be second, but in the upper stretch, War Admiral drew out to a three-length lead, doubling the margin he had enjoyed a quarter-mile or so before. Pompoon, who had broken from post position fourteen, retrieved more than a bit of his prestige by running second, although unable to challenge the winner. Reaping Reward was eight lengths farther back, but still got third money.

War Admiral's mile time had been 1:37 2/5, and he finished in 2:03 1/5. His jockey, "the Little Flying Dutchman," thus had for himself the unique distinction of having been aboard the winners of the two fastest Derbys on record, for the only one to better the time of War Admiral in a mile and one-quarter running of the race was Twenty Grand, who posted 2:01 4/5.

Despite their increasing connection as major targets, the relationship on the calendar of the Derby and Preakness was by no means fixed in 1937. The Preakness was up only a week later, and War Admiral cooled out of his Derby so well that he was placed onto a train car that very night and arrived at Baltimore, home of Pimlico and the Preakness, the next day. Celebrants and media would hardly know how to cope with such a sequence today, when one of the key moments to the entire Derby drama is the Sunday morning interview: The trainer is holding the reins as the new national hero grazes outside his/her barn at Churchill Downs, and it

often is discernible that the horse is less shaky than the horseman or the reporters as a result of their respective activities of the previous afternoon and night.

In the autumn of 2001, when Bob Baffert decided to run Officer in the California Cup only a week after his defeat in the Breeders' Cup Juvenile, he was castigated by more than a few of the Wise Men observing from the security of the press box. In 1937, after Conway had settled War Admiral in safely at Pimlico, he gave him an entire two more days before sending him out to work nine furlongs in 1:56 2/5. (Have horses really changed that much, or have trainers been hoodwinked — by outsiders and each other — or is another possibility that the concept of a "work" is more demanding today than before?)

On Wednesday morning of Preakness Week, War Admiral put in that move without being extended. Trainer C.F. Clarke worked Pompoon the same distance that morning. His recorded time was three-fifths of a second more than War Admiral's, but he finished under stout restraint, leaving the impression he would give a fine account of himself on Saturday.

War Admiral was favored at 35-100. Only two horses that had followed War Admiral at Churchill Downs had the appetite for more. Pompoon was one, and the other was Merry Maker, whose connections were able to convince themselves that his failure to get out of the ruck in one classic would be forgotten once he got to the muddy going expected at Pimlico. As it turned out, the track was labeled "good."

The field of eight also included War Admiral's former stablemate Over the Top, who was sold during the week of the Preakness to Mrs. W.H. Furst, while his former Faraway mate, Matey, was also entered. Matey and Wand, fellow members of the Man o' War triumvirate among 1936 juveniles, were destined to have disappointing campaigns at three, failing to live up to the sense of expectation they had created. Nevertheless, Matey was to be given his chance in the second of the Triple Crown classics.

Once again War Admiral was drawn on the rail, and once again he was responsible for a delay, as he "kept walking through the gate," as *The Blood-Horse* reported. Once again, too, he broke with the leaders, and Kurtsinger, as was his custom, put him on the lead. Still following the script from Louisville, he guided the colt out from the rail. He continued wide, find-ing firmer footing, despite losing ground on the turn, and settled into the backstretch comfortably in front. He had a length on Flying Scot, whose rider, Johnny Gilbert, had apparently observed that waiting and let-ting War Admiral have his way and then hoping to run him down were forlorn stratagems for victory. Wayne Wright had the same inclination, and he went ahead and moved Pompoon up to second, where he was sta-tioned, a length off the favorite, after six furlongs.

Stretch-long duels of two racehorses tend to create differing opinions, those observations often cast, com-fortably or not, in the terms of the individual observer's preconceived notions. In 1977 and 1978 it took many a withering stretch run in which Affirmed defeated Alydar for the proponents of the latter to begrudgingly admit that maybe their darling was second best. The Preakness of 1937 similarly teased Pompoon propo-nents into thinking, "Ah, at the longer distance of the Belmont, the Admiral belongs to us," while War Admiral fans were convinced that the closeness of the decision indicated a judicious use of the colt's superior-ity rather than a gaudy display of same.

At any rate, Pompoon came to the favorite turning for home, and they delighted the crowd of some 40,000 with a battle through the lane. War Admiral won by a head, and they had drawn eight lengths clear of third-placed Flying Scot. (Over the Top was fifth and Matey sixth.) The time for a mile and three-sixteenths was 1:58 2/5, which missed by only one-fifth of a second the stakes record set three years earlier by High Quest. (In a circumstance hardly fathomable in today's atmosphere of Triple Crown exultation, High Quest was urged to win by a head over his own stablemate, Cavalcade, even though the latter had won the Derby!)

The Blood-Horse's take on the stirring duel put War Admiral in his place in one sense of the word but recognized that it was really Pompoon who was destined to place: "Here War Admiral proved that he is no second Man o' War, (but) proved just as conclusively that he is Pompoon's master."

Hervey, in *American Race Horses of 1937*, quoted extensively from "notes on the race made at the time by a trained observer wholly disinterested." Ordinarily, we are wary of this concept, which journalists of today thrive on, i.e., "an unnamed source close to"

whomever. (The knee-jerk reaction in such cases is to wonder why the poor fellow's mother and father left him "unnamed;" but we digress.) However, the status as writer, historian, and horseman of John (Salvator) Hervey encourages a certain confidence. Either the following observations were his own personal ones, which he chose to relay by means of artifice, or he had confidence in some particular individual's powers of observation in the specialized exercise of watching a horse race in a day before instant replay:

"I was sitting about the middle of the stretch and the whole thing happened at the home turn. Coming into it, Pompoon was moving up on War Admiral, having been previously about a length and a half behind him. In rounding it, Kurtsinger took the Admiral out very wide, either because he thought he could carry Pompoon out, or because he had been taking all the turns very wide — I understand, to get out in better footing. Pompoon did not really close on War Admiral. Instead, Wright cut over very sharply to the rail, and thereby saved Pompoon a length and a half in no time. In other words; instead of being a length and a half behind him, he was within a nose of the Admiral. So they came down the stretch, Pompoon being driven and whipped and answering very gamely, Kurtsinger sitting very snugly on his colt, just once waving his whip in front of his eyes but never striking him. As I saw the race, Kurtsinger nearly threw it away by taking the last turn so very wide, then retrieved himself by not losing his head coming down the stretch. If Pompoon hadn't saved so much ground on that last turn, he would have been just about the same number of lengths behind at the end as he was in the Derby."

Owner Riddle was able to witness the Preakness, accepting the historic Woodlawn Vase, and he was also at Belmont Park three weeks later for the denouement of American racing's fourth Triple Crown.

One of the enjoyments of following, or reporting on, racehorses is to try prematurely to place them in perspective while hastening to suggest that the exercise is, indeed, premature. Joe Palmer, one of the most graceful and knowledgeable of Turf writers, reveled in this in the weeks between the second classic and the third:

"It is practically second guessing to predict that War Admiral will win the Belmont Stakes, or any other 3-year-old event, if he retains his form. In fact,

most contemporary argument centers over whether the speedy brown colt is the best son which Man o' War has sent to the races. A few persons ventured to remark that he was 'another Man o' War,' but were more or less promptly scoffed out of court. But the experts have stopped racing War Admiral against Pompoon, Brooklyn, et. al., and have begun matching him with Crusader. It is very difficult to deny that the comparison, so far, is in favor of the current 3-year-old champion. After all, when a horse does all that is asked of him, as War Admiral has done in four starts this year, he belongs close to the top."

A sentence or two later, Palmer reversed his field: "But it is not amiss to recall that Crusader, while not a Derby contender, had no mean turn of speed himself...

"With all credit to the performances of Pompoon, Flying Scot, Reaping Reward, and others which have met War Admiral this year, I am very much mistaken if they reach, collectively, the calibre of Crusader's opponents. War Admiral may be Man o' War's best son, but he has several tests to pass before this becomes indisputable."

A very important one of those tests, of course, lay just ahead.

The last trainer we personally recall working a Belmont candidate the entire mile and one-half of the classic in preparation was John Veitch, who grew up under the tutelage of his father, Hall of Famer Syl Veitch. The elder Veitch's career as a trainer of major winners reached back nearly to the War Admiral days. The younger Veitch sent his vaunted Alydar out for a mile and one-half before his epic, although barely unsuccessful, effort against Affirmed in 1978. In 1937 Conway punctuated the three weeks between the Preakness and Belmont not with a single work of the entire Belmont route, but with three such trips!

The first was accomplished in 2:36 2/5; the second, in 2:34 3/5. Then, on Wednesday before the race itself, he did a repeat mile and one-half in an identical 2:34 3/5.

On May 30, Pompoon worked the full Belmont distance in 2:35, and then the next day, Sceneshifter got the route in 2:33 in his own workout. Even more spectacular was the apparently rejuvenated Brooklyn, who scorched the route in 2:31 4/5. Brooklyn had failed to train satisfactorily coming up to the Derby, but Bradley and Pompoon's owner, Louchheim, had struck again their one-on-one bet for the Belmont. If time were

taken as a point-blank evaluation, Brooklyn's work would have won six of the eleven Belmonts since the race was adjusted to a mile and one-half in 1926.

A crowd estimated at 35,000 turned up to see a field of seven set out on the final journey of the Triple. Legal bookmaking still prevailed in New York at the time, and the odds on War Admiral were said to be 4-5, while Pompoon was 3-1 and Brooklyn 6-1. War Admiral, having lived with the inside post in the Derby and Preakness, this time was drawn on the outside. Once again, he held up the start, dashing prematurely through his door in the old open-gate system. It is only fair to say he was not the only one who cut up rough and delayed the start for about eight minutes. At the final break, however, he was his own victim, for while he bolted away alertly, he also was in such a hurry that, as Hervey described it, he "struck the quarter of his right fore-foot and sheared off it, as with a knife, a portion of the wall of the hoof an inch or more square, leaving a gaping wound from which blood was flowing." Some reports had it that the break was so unsettled that, for a moment, Kurtsinger thought his dear little champion was going down.

There is irony that the phrase "hot-blooded" can be perceived as a positive, when the physical reality is that a hasty horse can slash one eager leg with another. Now, a unique drama had been preordained, and War Admiral went about his Belmont as if the smell, and feel, of blood-letting aroused him to supreme effort.

With a quarter-mile spurt in :24, he had a three-length lead, and he put another panel on that margin as he toured a half-mile in :48. John Hay Whitney's Flying Scot retreated after chasing the Admiral that far and was replaced as runner-up by Sceneshifter. After nine furlongs War Admiral had a lead of four lengths on Sceneshifter, and none of the others could come forward even enough to displace the second.

The furlongs rattled by, the blood spiraling with every stride and clinging to the underbelly of a wild and lovely beast. A mile in 1:37 1/5 was three-fifths of a second faster than Snark's Metropolitan Mile that spring; a mile and one-quarter in 2:02 1/5 was swifter than War Admiral's own Kentucky Derby; a mile and three-furlongs in 2:15 2/5 bettered Sir Barton's time back when the race ended at that point, and, finally, the entire mile and one-half in 2:28 3/5 was a new stakes and track

record. The previous track record for Belmont Park had been set by War Admiral's sire, Man o' War, at 2:28 4/5 in the 1920 Jockey Club Gold Cup. War Admiral's final clocking equaled the American record, set ten years earlier by Handy Mandy in the Latonia Derby.

Sceneshifter persevered to remain second, finishing three lengths back, while Vamoose was third, ten lengths farther in arrears. Brooklyn was fourth, to win Colonel Bradley's desultory bet (although he was winless in four races that year), while Pompoon came back lame after finishing sixth.

Hervey pulled no punches in describing War Admiral's injury: "Every time his foot struck the track it had caused the blood to spurt from the wound, and the under side of his body was dyed with it. That, under such circumstances, he should have run the record-making race he did was testimony of a gameness difficult to extol too highly."

Equally impressed at the show of courage was a young artist who years later recalled the scene in the introduction to a book on his own career:

"A little brown horse raced through the stretch at Belmont Park one June afternoon more than a half-century ago...From a personal point of view, he was racing solidly into my life as well, and the image he left with me that afternoon has never waned."

The memory was that of the artist Richard Stone Reeves (*Legends*, Oxmoor House, 1989), who was seventeen years old at the time and who in a distinguished career since then has painted countless Thoroughbred champions of the United States and Europe. "How often I have thought back to that day. Here was the embodiment of so much that has meant everything to my professional career: The wonderful creature that is the Thoroughbred...adding to the visual and emotional impact War Admiral thrust upon me that June day was his own literal 'red badge of courage.' Even today, one never reads or hears of the 1937 Belmont without the addendum that War Admiral injured himself at the gate and bled from the wound for the entire 1 1/2 miles of the race...he came back to the winner's circle spurting blood from what must have been a painful, alarming injury. And yet, War Admiral had never wavered from his task..."

(Perhaps the budding artist was meant all along to be inspired by War Admiral. After all, when the colt's sire, Man o' War, was purchased on behalf of Sam Riddle as a yearling, the representative doing the actual bidding was one Mr. Ed Buhler — an uncle of the self-same Richard Stone Reeves!)

Owner Riddle descended to the winner's circle, where he was met by the widow of Man o' War's breeder. In addition to handing Kurtsinger and Riddle the scalloped silver Belmont Stakes tray, Mrs. Belmont also donated the massive bowl still emblematic of the stakes, i.e., the trophy originally awarded her late husband's father for Fenian's victory in the 1869 Belmont Stakes.

Not seen in old photographs of the ceremony was trainer Conway, who had immediately sought veterinary advice. The injury was deemed serious, but not career ending. In the Shakespearean tension of emotions, the sunshine of victory was "sicklied o'er by the pale cast" of reality in Conway's comment that "I don't see how he can be brought back to the races before fall, and even that is doubtful."

Still, the little Admiral had won the Triple Crown!

CHAPTER 5

Horse Of The Year

For the second year in a row, War Admiral was unable to race at that garden of earthly delights known as Saratoga. He recovered from his injury in time to train there, however, and on August 14 he appeared publicly under silks as an added highlight to the Travers Stakes Day. (Burning Star won the Travers over Up and Doing, with Matey running third.)

By late September, he was shipped to Maryland, where Conway was almost ready to run him several times before actually sending him to the post on October 26. Thus, more than four and a half months had passed between his Belmont and his comeback. Conway had found an allowance race that, incredibly, let War Admiral in with 106 pounds — twenty less than he had carried in the Triple Crown. Despite the favorable weight, though, the assignment was far from easy.

He was going a mile and one-sixteenth at Laurel for a purse of $1,200, and the seven horses aligned against him included the accomplished Aneroid, winner of four major stakes triumphs that year, including the Suburban Handicap. The older horse was carrying 113 pounds.

Despite the layoff and quality of opponent, War Admiral was sent away at 2-5. As if nothing untoward had befallen the colt, Kurtsinger put him right on the lead, and they had a three-length lead at the first call. This he continued to hold, at one point drawing out by an additional length, and he won easily by two and a half lengths in 1:46. Aneroid was second, and third was the filly Floradora, winner of the Alabama Stakes and Maryland Handicap the previous year.

In those days the late fall meetings in Maryland constituted the final segment of the major Eastern season and were more or less on par with the New York circuit. Conway felt War Admiral was now ready to go back to the sternest tests available, and only four days after the allowance race, War Admiral contested the $15,000 Washington Handicap. For the first time in a drama that would go on for a year, the possibility arose that War Admiral might meet Seabiscuit.

Charles S. Howard's Seabiscuit, purchased as something of a castoff from Wheatley Stable, was becoming a public idol, much in the way John Henry did many years later. He was of modest breeding (although his sire, Hard Tack, was a son of Man o' War), and he earned his way into the hearts of the public as he climbed the ranks and won stakes after stakes across the country. California racing had only recently been renewed, and Easterners tended to think that if Seabiscuit could win major races out there the quality must be a bit below that of New York and Maryland. This was based on the mistaken thought that the Seabiscuit they were hearing about was the same horse they had seen run through thirty-five races at two, with only modest results. Like John Henry, though, Seabiscuit had improved enough with age that he was now of national championship caliber.

By the autumn of 1937, Seabiscuit at four had won the San Juan Capistrano and Bay Meadows on the West Coast, but had also knocked down a series of the tougher pins on the East Coast, to wit, the Massachusetts Handicap, Brooklyn Handicap, and Butler Handicap. All told, he won ten stakes that year

and was War Admiral's primary foe in the newish game of Horse of the Year balloting.

As October waned, Seabiscuit, too, was on the grounds at Laurel and was eligible for the Washington. The older horse was assigned 130 pounds; the younger colt 126. Scale weight for a mile and one-quarter at that time of year called for a three-year-old to receive six pounds from a four-year-old. Thus, the weight assignment for the Washington Handicap was a small compliment to War Admiral. As it turned out, Seabiscuit was not entered. He had missed a work because of the rain, and Howard and trainer Tom Smith doubted his readiness to run his best over the heavy footing that would prevail.

Nevertheless, War Admiral faced a stern task, for he was giving a pound of actual weight, and seven pounds by scale, to Aneroid and as much as seventeen pounds by scale to five others. Still, he was bet down to nearly 3-5. Again, he dominated from early on, taking the lead in the first one hundred yards and opening a three-length lead. Through the stretch, he eased off and allowed the three-year-old Heelfly (119) to close the gap to a length and a half. The chart, for the third straight race, used the term "easily."

The victory increased War Admiral's earnings for the year to $160,820. (The mathematics of the earnings list was the only theater of combat for War Admiral and Seabiscuit that year, and the older horse eventually won that nominal contest.) War Admiral came out again four days later for the $7,500 Pimlico Special. The mile and three-sixteenths race was then for three-year-olds only, and with his own weight up to 128 pounds, War Admiral was giving from nineteen to twenty-eight pounds to three rivals. He was sent off at 1-20. In his only earlier start over the Pimlico strip, he had had his one close race of the year, and it had been suggested, but not universally assumed, that this, in part, had to do with a dislike of the footing. The 1937 Pimlico Special added credibility to that notion. If this were a warning to his owner and trainer, it was one they either did not heed or felt they could not act upon, for when he finally got his duel with Seabiscuit, it would be in the same race (with conditions altered) over the same track the following year!

In the 1937 Special, War Admiral struggled at the start and was unable to take the lead and dominate. He was already under pressure to take second by shaking

clear of War Minstrel (109) and Bottle Cap (107) on the backstretch. The feather-weighted Masked General (100) was up ahead, alone on the lead, and War Admiral took out after him, being already under the whip with a half-mile to run. Writing of the race in the *Bloodstock Breeders' Review*, Neil Newman took the position that "it appeared as if his weight would render his efforts fruitless."

At the turn, however, War Admiral was assigned the opposite role from that he carried out in the Preakness. This time it was he who hugged the rail while Masked General bolted wide. Kurtsinger got War Admiral to even terms, and then the gallant little colt drew out to win by a length and a half. It was his third race in nine days and elicited the comment "won driving." The time was 1:58 4/5. Whatever his degree of discomfort on the Pimlico track might have been, he had come within four-fifths of a second of the track record in order to do what he always avidly wanted to do — outrun everything else on the track. Masked General was not yet a stakes winner but was rounding into a form that would see him win several important Mid-Atlantic handicaps in later years, among them the Washington, Philadelphia, and Sussex handicaps.

Thus, War Admiral had won all eight of his races at three and had earned $166,500. That he showed the grit to overcome the difficulties and weight concessions — with perhaps a bit of good luck — to preserve victory in the Pimlico Special was probably vital to his prevailing as Horse of the Year in the second year of the *Daily Racing Form* ballot. In the poll of another publication of the day, *Turf & Sport Digest*, War Admiral was also named Horse of the Year, although the honor was afforded Seabiscuit in yet another selection, that of the magazine *Horse & Horsemen*. Historically, the *Daily Racing Form* version of the election has been accorded the highest credibility, in part perhaps because of that publication's continued prominence.

Seabiscuit wound up the leading earner for the season with $168,580, having won eleven of fifteen in the handicap division. His owner of record, Mrs. Charles S. Howard, led the owners' list with $214,559. (Following Mrs. Isabel Dodge Sloane's Brookmeade Stable and Mrs. Ethel V. Mars' Milky Way Stable, Mrs. Howard technically became the third woman in four years to top that list, although by all accounts her husband was far more involved in the workings of the stable. When

War Admiral, a diminutive brown colt, didn't resemble his famous sire, the big chestnut Man o' War, but the son inherited the father's ability as well as his fierce desire to win.

Through his grandsire Fair Play (above) and sire, the legendary Man o' War (right), War Admiral was a product of the fiery Hastings line. War Admiral's broodmare sire Sweep (below right) provided solid American bloodlines through daughter Brushup (below).

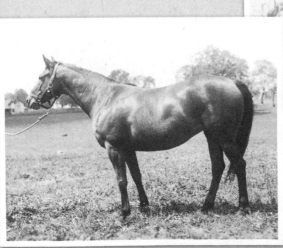

Owner-breeder Samuel D. Riddle (left) was initially unimpressed with his brown Man o' War colt, but under trainer George Conway's tutelage (above), War Admiral flourished. Charley Kurtsinger (top left) was the Admiral's regular rider.

Conway watched War Admiral (above in lead) warm up for morning excercise. The dog at Conway's feet was War Admiral's pet and acted as stable watch dog. The Admiral won one stakes at two before starting his three-year-old season with two wins at Havre de Grace, including the Chesapeake Stakes (below).

After his Chesapeake victory, War Admiral went right into the Kentucky Derby, only his second time going beyond a mile. He won (below) by one and three-quarters lengths and garnered the roses for Riddle and Conway (right). Seven days later War Admiral was back in action in the Preakness and held off Pompoon to win by a head (top).

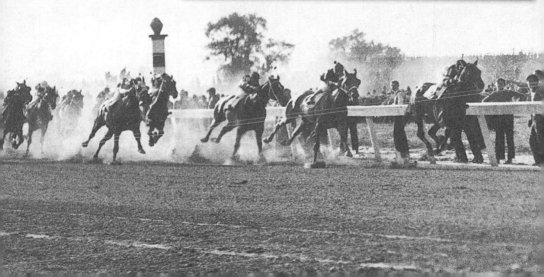

At the start of the Belmont Stakes, War Admiral badly cut his right front foot and ran injured the entire way to win by three lengths (below). Conway brought the courageous colt (right) back to the winner's circle where Riddle (below right, on the far left) received the trophy from Mrs. August Belmont, the widow of Man o' War's breeder.

War Admiral's foot injury prevented him from making the races at Saratoga that summer, but he did parade at the racetrack on Travers Day (left, with Conway and Mrs. Samuel Riddle). He returned to the races in October of 1937 with an allowance victory. He then easily won the Washington Handicap at Laurel (below) and the Pimlico Special. In his first outing at four, War Admiral captured an allowance at Hialeah (above).

War Admiral wintered with Conway's stable in Florida (below). Taking a string of horses south was a relatively new tradition among prominent racing stables. The Admiral worked at Hialeah (right) in preparation for his major goal, the Widener Cup, which he won with little trouble (above).

In 1938 War Admiral finally managed to race at Saratoga. He didn't disappoint, winning all four starts there, including the Saratoga Handicap (left), Whitney (below), and Saratoga Cup (bottom).

War Admiral next dominated at Belmont Park with a three-length victory in the Jockey Club Gold Cup (above). His trip to the winner's circle (top) was the eighth in nine outings to that point in his four-year-old season.

While War Admiral was conquering the East, Seabiscuit had become the West's hero. Riddle and Seabiscuit's owner, C.S. Howard (right, on the left), agreed to a match race. War Admiral lived up to his fiery nature at a publicity shoot (below) for the first match, planned for May 30, which fell through. He was on his best behavior in late October (above with Riddle) as a second attempt at a match race loomed.

The match race between War Admiral and Seabiscuit was set for November 1, 1938, in the Pimlico Special. The Admiral (above) and the Biscuit (below) showed off in workouts at Pimlico.

War Admiral led Seabiscuit to the post (above) for the Pimlico Special, but Seabiscuit was in front at the wire.

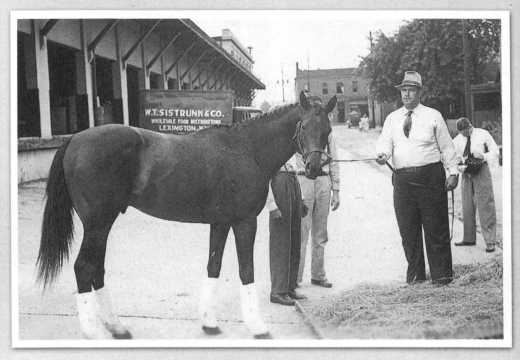

War Admiral came back to win his final two races before being retired and sent to Lexington, Kentucky, for stud duty (above). War Admiral entered stud at Riddle's Faraway Farm, where his famous father still stood. A mature stallion, the Admiral posed in 1944 with Will Harbut (below), the groom who also cared for Man o' War.

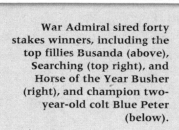

War Admiral sired forty
stakes winners, including the
top fillies Busanda (above),
Searching (top right), and
Horse of the Year Busher
(right), and champion two-
year-old colt Blue Peter
(below).

In 1958, seven years after Riddle's death, War Admiral was moved from Faraway Farm to young Preston Madden's Hamburg Place east of Lexington (above, Madden on far right). War Admiral stood one season there before his death in 1959. The little brown son of Man o' War was buried near his sire's statue at Faraway. The graves of War Admiral and Man o' War now lie at the Kentucky Horse Park.

WAR ADMIRAL
BY MAN O' WAR
OUT OF BRUSHUP
FOALED 1934
DIED 1959

TRIPLE CROWN WINNER
1937

the stable topped the earnings list again in 1940, the horses ran in the husband's name, so that the Howards officially had his and her titles as leading owner.)

Seabiscuit was ridden throughout that year only by Red Pollard, but Kurtsinger won the jockeys' money-winning title with $384,202. In addition to War Admiral's many victories, Kurtsinger's other stakes triumphs included a score in the rich Futurity on Hal Price Headley's Menow. Later events would reveal a certain irony to that connection.

Of War Admiral, Hervey at year's end rhapsodized that, "It seems no exaggeration to state that no colt seen in this country since Man o' War, seventeen years ago, has made so deep an impression." In this assertion he would have been at odds with the most adamant fans of the 1930 Triple Crown winner, Gallant Fox, including the latter's owner and breeder, William Woodward Sr. Woodward, in fact, had authored a Gallant Fox book in which he mused how his colt stacked up against Man o' War. Nevertheless, it is not to be doubted that War Admiral had, indeed, earned enormous respect.

Hervey continued: "His sequence of...victories, his

wonderfully attractive individuality — for the public always rises to a great 'little'un' with a peculiar fervor — his extraordinary speed and his way of going at once to the front and then staying there; his gameness and consistency, and the fact of his paternity, all combined to win for him an admiration such as few race horses have aroused.

"If he disclosed a fault, as a performer, it was his restiveness at the post. Like his sire he seems burning to be off and away once he reaches the starting point, while, as do many other horses, he bitterly dislikes the stalls. Otherwise, he is a faultless racing machine. Though so highly organized he can be placed and rated, he runs without hood (blinkers)."

He added that Riddle had refused an offer of $250,000 and intended to stand the horse at Faraway Farm whenever he was retired. Insofar as such evaluations can be reduced to dollars, this would indicate the gulf that remained between the prestige of Man o' War and all other horses, for owner Riddle years before had famously spurned an offer of four times that much for the older horse.

Riddle authored the foreword for Hervey's volume

Race Horses of 1937, and he touched upon the starting gates of the day in a general way:

"We have had one improvement at our race track that we should all be very glad to have. We have now with us the photographic finish. It is marvelous. It solves a large problem for us. If we can only in some way have the walk-up start, it would be a great help. It takes too long to get horses off in the old-fashioned way. The public would not stand for it today. No doubt, we will evolve some plan that will give us better starting than we have now, which is even a pleasure to anticipate."

Riddle was looking forward to the day that there would be something beyond the older era's often rambunctious walk-up start and the development of open starting gates that made possible such phrases as "whisked in and out of his stall persistently." The current starting gates, long ago adopted, with enclosed stall and synchronized opening of front doors, generally would be regarded as an improvement, although War Admiral might well have created even more of a tempest!

In addition to Hervey, others who extolled the degree to which War Admiral had gained celebrity was John Kieran, who after the Triple Crown had devoted a

column in *The New York Times* to the young champion.
This column stressed the impact of the colt not merely
on the Turf, but upon the general public, a sentiment
that correlates to the often expressed need for "a hero"
by those seeking to promote Thoroughbred racing in
the twenty-first century.

Kieran wrote:

"The records have it that Samuel D. Riddle is the
sole owner of War Admiral. But the elderly owner of
Faraway Farm, where the great Man o' War grazes in
green pastures, would be the first to admit that his sole
ownership of War Admiral may be fairly open to dispute.
The public now has a big interest in the little horse...

"The racing regulars need no help around a track,
but a horse like War Admiral is a boon to innocent
bystanders and casual visitors. They don't have to
study charts or tune in on stable gossip or paddock
chatter to know about War Admiral. Why, they even
know a little about Pompoon now...

"The political economists have been debating public
ownership in their realm for some centuries, but in the
realm of sport the matter is swiftly settled. The public
moves right in and takes possession. When a Man o'

War or a Sun Beau or a Stromboli comes along on the Turf, various owners or breeders may show bills of sale or breeding records to prove legal title, but that's just legal fiction. Man o' War was everybody's horse. So was Stromboli and Eternal and Sysonby and Phar Lap.

"Now, it's War Admiral. Owned by Glen Riddle Farm, is he? Well, Mr. Riddle is a grand old gentleman and nobody would want to put him into a temper. But when War Admiral ambles out under silks, just watch the spectators in the stands or on the lawn. The pride of ownership is in their eyes. That's their horse! It's nice to have Mr. Riddle pay the bills for his upkeep and it's good to have a genial gent like the veteran trainer, George Conway, looking after him. But when they turn him loose and send him to the races War Admiral belongs to the public.

"It is not only a matter of public ownership but also of public benefit. Take an ordinary tourist and lead him to a race track. He's bewildered. It's a pretty sight — the gay grandstand, the racing strip, the flowers and trees and music and chatter, but then the horses start to run and it's all confusion to him. Most of the horses look alike. Some win, some lose. What of it?"

Great horses and great events, such as the Zev-Papyrus international match, the coming of Phar Lap, Kieran went on with stunning hyperbole "help the blind...to those ignorant of the everyday details of racing, the secrets of form charts, the differences in conditions and weights and jockeys and fast or slow tracks, great horses are lights in the darkness. They rouse the torpid to a feeling of enthusiasm. They do well for their owners, but they do better for the Turf as a sport. Horses like these are more than animated gambling devices...

"Now it's a son of Man o' War who has come galloping to glory. War Admiral must be a great horse, a little fellow with a big heart. There is such a thing as racing luck, to be sure. There are bad breaks at the barrier and interference along the way. All horses run into that sooner or later if they stay long enough where the going is fast and furious.

"But no luck ever carried a horse to victory in those three races in one year, the Kentucky Derby, the Preakness and the Belmont. Luck doesn't stretch that far or last that long...It is to be hoped that the land-going War Admiral, sound as a dollar, will soon be back under silks, commanding the admiration that everybody gives to a great competitor in any sport and rousing the spirit of public ownership that everybody feels in a great horse."

CHAPTER 6

'Applauded to the Echo'

Patterns of American Thoroughbred racing, for the most part, have been subject to change. The image of the Turf is one of unswerving devotion to the strictures and traditions that have gone before, but that image is a canard. War Admiral was involved in one of those sequences that dictate the perceived certitudes of one era will be scuttled by the fashion of the next. Nothing in Sam Riddle's sporting proclivities, be it hunting fox and coon in Pennsylvania and Maryland or serving juleps and mining yearlings in Saratoga, had prepared him for the concept that fashionable Thoroughbred stables should court the alligators and herons of southern Florida. Yet, by the time War Admiral's three-year-old season was ready to segue into his handicap-racing season, winter in Florida had burst upon the scene of the nation's sporting calendar. The importance of Hialeah, and then Gulfstream, would dictate a Florida commencement of many championship campaigns over the years.

Several seasons would yet pass before trainer Ben A. Jones wintered Whirlaway in South Florida for that nascent empire of American racing, Calumet Farm. That year, 1941, Jones famously nudged the colt along the Triple Crown path. In 1938, however, the self-same Jones had been plowing the seeds of Florida's winter fashion in his management of Woolford Farm's Lawrin, who was destined to become the trainer's first Derby winner. Meanwhile, the sportsman Joseph E. Widener, a key investor in the floral chateau that was Hialeah, had redrawn the lines of winter plans for important stables. Whether Philadelphia's shared importance to Widener's and Riddle's social hierarchies was relevant to War Admiral's plans, we cannot say. Nevertheless, the very year that the outspoken Ben A. Jones was readying his first Derby winner along the southern shores of eastern Florida, the stolid George Conway was soon to be there, too, confronting the massive public interest in the return to action of a Triple Crown winner.

The key target on the West Coast was the $100,000

Santa Anita Handicap, inaugurated three years before. In Florida its counterpart was the Widener. Begun as the Widener Challenge Cup in 1936, the race had carried a purse of $10,150 for its first winner, Mantagna. Then, in 1937, the purse had been elevated to such extreme that the filly Columbiana earned $52,000 for her victory. By its third running, the race was known as the Widener Cup Handicap, and War Admiral was assigned 130 pounds for the $50,000-added event. There was no doubt that it was one of those races that are created one day and are rapidly encased within the schedule of the important races of the Turf. (Those of more recent generations can easily understand such a phenomenon as comparable to the immediate importance of such races as the Marlboro Cup, Arlington Million, and Breeders' Cups.)

Previous Riddle stars had had a leisurely spring stay at Berlin prescribed for them. With the Widener set for March 5, 1938, however, trainer Conway had no such luxury of schedule. Riddle had been induced to enter War Admiral in the Santa Anita Handicap in its earliest nomination stage, but the colt was put on a train headed to Florida. War Admiral was still techni-

cally a three-year-old when he arrived at Hialeah, on New Year's Eve.

The glare of the spotlight would be upon him on any occasion that Conway assayed the colt's sunrise passages between the barns and the racecourse. On the opposite coast, trainer Tom Smith was facing an identical situation with Seabiscuit. Both trainers also faced the common question of when, and under what conditions, should we venture out for a prep race?

On several occasions War Admiral was intended to run prior to the mile and one-quarter Widener, but that persnickety old fox Sam Riddle did not want to accept a burden of 130 pounds in a tune-up when that was also the prescribed weight for the main target. The owner famously was caught in a quote involving those whose job it is to assign weights, to wit, "All the handicappers know about a horse is that one end bites and the other end kicks."

So, the strategy languished, and Conway did not send War Admiral out for his four-year-old debut until February 19. The vehicle was a seven-furlong event in which he carried 122 pounds, giving from six to twelve pounds to five rivals. He was bet down at 3-10. One wants a hint of perfection in such circumstances, but War Admiral decided to add to his reputation as a difficult gate horse. Indeed, his antics at the start prompted the starter to decree that the colt was not fit for the gate — or vice versa — but must make his way from outside the stalls. War Admiral found this acceptable and scooted away near the front. He had seldom allowed a mere horse to take the lead, and this gate incident was not enough to furl the Admiral's standard, even for the moment.

Kurtsinger had him four lengths in front at one time, and they reined in to win by a comfortable length and a half over Sir Oracle (116) in 1:23 4/5.

The colt's fame was such that Conway was induced to delay daily training until the afternoon and bring him out before the Hialeah crowd. On February 26 matters were becoming serious enough that War Admiral dashed a mile in 1:39 1/5 in the last of these matinee larks. In less public circumstances, he went through what was often known as his "distance trial," the full mile and one-quarter Widener route in 2:06 on March 1. Then, on March 4, the day before the race, Conway dusted off any hidden cobwebs of idleness by sending the colt a half-mile in :50 2/5.

Thus, on March 5, four months after his most recent important test, the champion of one year was ready to implant his superiority onto the next. A crowd of 21,000 made their way to be witnesses.

As mentioned earlier, the $100,000 Santa Anita Handicap and $50,000 Widener Handicap went off on the same day in 1938. If two such champions could be mustered for concurrent races today, it would be expected that both would face small fields, each likely comprising allowance horses whose trainers and owners had spotted a keen spot for decent place money. In 1938, however, the economics of the game were such that seventeen horses faced Seabiscuit and twelve sallied against War Admiral.

Nevertheless, War Admiral under 130 pounds was intimidating to the point that he was less than 4-5 while conceding from thirteen to twenty-eight pounds. Again, his shenanigans had him relegated to a place outside the starting gate, but he looked upon such gentle banishment as no more than an inconvenience, if that, and took Kurtsinger on his accustomed dash to the front. Temerity brought a sequence of pretenders to within a length: Piccolo second after a quarter-mile, Bourbon King second after six furlongs. Thereafter, War Admiral shooed off this sort and led by three lengths after a mile, five lengths after a mile and one-eighth. With Kurtsinger tugging against him, War Admiral scored by a length and a half. Zevson (104) rallied from eleventh at 41-1 odds to secure a moment in runner-up history, while War Minstrel (111) was third as part of a 35-1 entry. The time of 2:03 4/5 was given more specific context by Hervey's explanation that after the 1936 and 1937 Widener winners' shared mark of 2:01 4/5, "the Hialeah track had been resurfaced and considerably slowed in the process, this being done because of the criticisms that its previous great speed was due to an insufficient cushion, hard on the legs and feet of horses racing over it."

Conway had survived the oddity of wintering in Florida and had accomplished his goal of winning the Widener. Within forty-eight hours he had hustled horse and self back to Maryland, where instead of winter quarters he would enjoy "spring quarters" while awaiting Riddle's decision on what challenges he would accept next. This was no clear-cut matter, and Riddle

was of two minds. On the one hand, he apparently felt as the proprietor of the national champion he had the trump card in the game of owner versus handicapper. Like many a horseman before and since, he decried the circumstance of his poor little horse facing increasing weights were he to accept them in the spring and summer handicaps. On the other hand, he had been conditioned from the days of Man o' War's career to understand that ownership of such a horse bore a public responsibility, as well. Then, too, there was the growing and restless clamor for a meeting with Seabiscuit.

Howard's older star had lost the Santa Anita Handicap on the day War Admiral won the Widener, but Seabiscuit's performance had been so noble that the loss did nothing to scuff the patina of his national glamour. He was beaten by Stagehand. In an audacious early season challenge of older horses, three-year-old Stagehand had won by a nose, carrying one hundred pounds to Seabiscuit's 130!

In her milestone 2001 bestseller *Seabiscuit, An American Legend* (Random House), Laura Hillenbrand observed poignantly that as early as the previous year, "A single thought occupied the minds of everyone in racing. Seabiscuit and War Admiral had to meet."

By the winter of 1938, when both had acquitted themselves nobly in their key winter targets, Hillenbrand pointed out, Howard recognized that the field of play as it was presented — or perceived — cast him in the role of having something to prove: "Like Riddle, he understood that Seabiscuit had to conquer War Admiral on the track to be deemed his superior in the championship voting and in history. With so much riding on the meeting, he and (trainer Tom) Smith did not want their horse to meet War Admiral in a full-field race, in which he would run the risk of a horse interfering with him..." It was ordained, then, that a match race should be the vehicle for the two public stars' clash.

Herbert Bayard Swope, the long-time chairman of the New York Racing Commission, was asked by Howard to try to arrange such a race. Swope countered with the idea of inducing Belmont Park to raise the purse of its Suburban Handicap from $20,000 to $50,000. As Hillenbrand recorded, Howard did not view that as ideal, but realized it was logical to play along, or at least seem to do so.

Hialeah's Joseph E. Widener also was an important figure in the Belmont Park board room, and he agreed to the new ante. At that point, Howard must have figured the trump card was in his hand, for he recast the scenario, calling for double the purse for less of a race, to wit, $100,000 not for the Suburban but for a two-horse match. Swope duly approached Belmont with that new deal. Widener needed the acquiescence of another of the key members of the board of Westchester Racing Association, which then operated Belmont Park, and that individual, C.V. Whitney, was away on a fishing trip.

Playing poker with Sam Riddle was no easy thing. Riddle made noises about how the splashy Chicago track, Arlington Park, was also on board for a $100,000 race, so maybe it would be a good idea to have the horses meet twice. Clearly, in such a scenario, Belmont as host of merely the first of two races would find its position of eminence lessened. Howard was aware of Riddle's concern about War Admiral's carrying too much weight and agreed to run at any weight, winner-take-all, at a mile and one-quarter.

At length, the deal was struck, and Whitney gave his

okay, albeit reluctantly. War Admiral and Seabiscuit would meet in a match race at Belmont Park on Memorial Day, May 30. The race would have a purse of $100,000, and the weight for each was 126 pounds over ten furlongs.

Much later, it was often implied by the press retrospectively that War Admiral was generally seen as the classier of the two. However, as the May 30 date approached, various articles in the racing press stressed that by then any failure to appreciate Seabiscuit's quality had long since been washed away by his unceasing accomplishments. Writer Charles Hatton quoted the noted bookmaker (bookmaking was still legal in New York) Tom Shaw as suggesting the odds would likely be 3-5 War Admiral, 7-5 Seabiscuit, but that if the race were in California instead, they would be "Even Stephen." More significantly, Shaw expected Seabiscuit to win, Hatton said, quoting the bookmaker that "if Seabiscuit is ever within a length and a half of War Admiral he will win it sure."

Nelson Dunstan began a column in which he called himself "one of the minority who concede Seabiscuit a good chance in the match race on May 30," and

he opined that War Admiral had demonstrated courage only once, in his Preakness against Pompoon,
whereas Seabiscuit had passed several "landmarks of
his courage." Dunstan was perhaps not accurate in
placing himself on such a lonely island. In addition to
Shaw's compliance, Bud Stotler, trainer of the great
Discovery for Alfred Vanderbilt, was quoted that "with
only two starting he won't have much difficulties and
I firmly believe he's a gamer horse than War Admiral."
Columnist Fred Keats noted what he saw as a confus-
ing circumstance, but one that recognized the respect
Seabiscuit had engendered: "A peculiar feature of the
special race between War Admiral and Seabiscuit is
that while the figures of every speed handicapper in the
land point to Seabiscuit, War Admiral is a strong favorite in the betting. Bookmakers are cold-blooded lads
and usually go with the figures. This time, they are on
the other side of the fence with the rest of the crowd."

As the public waited, and thousands of dollars
worth of extra trains and private parties were eagerly
thrown together, rumors suggesting less than perfection in each horse made their maddening rounds. Six
days before the race, the rumors relative to Seabiscuit

proved founded, and Smith and Howard had to inform the Belmont officials that their horse could not fulfill the engagement. Sadly, Howard recognized, a year and more worth of lingering snide comment from some corners that the horse was not genuine enough to challenge a proven Eastern champion would seem justified. It was inaccurate, but there was nothing he could do.

Belmont had moved the Suburban from May 30 to May 28. Once the match was cancelled, Riddle entered War Admiral in the handicap, although he had been assigned 132 pounds. Riddle was sick in bed at home again. As reported in *American Race Horses of 1938*, rain during the night and early morning prompted Conway to scratch War Admiral, although by the time the Suburban was run the track was swift enough to accede to a new stakes record. Conway's announcement came late, with a huge crowd in attendance. The scratching was met with understandable frustration and venting of disgust. After all, the racing public for weeks had been titillated to a degree beyond exaggeration, only to be disappointed, and now another, albeit lesser, blow had been delivered.

Whitney was furious. "This is an outrage," he said,

"and I want it clearly understood that Belmont Park had nothing to do with it. When the match race was called off, we had Mr. Riddle's definite assurance that he would start his horse in the Suburban…I am terribly hurt and am just as helpless. Thousands came here today to see that horse run, but their disappointment is sharper than mine…This is the result of a situation caused by that match race." Reporter Murray Tynan added that Whitney was then asked if he would ever approve a match race again, and the young sportsman continued his heartfelt expressing of himself: "Not if I could buy them for a dime a dozen. If anyone wants to run a match race here again, they'll do it on their own and with their own money. I'll never again consent to such a thing, and I was opposed to it from the start. I gave in, I'll admit, and see what has happened."

(Had War Admiral contested the Suburban, it would have found him against old foes. Among the beaten field were Aneroid and Pompoon as Wheatley Stable's Snark won in 2:01 2/5, the fastest time for a mile and one-quarter race for the year.)

Apparently, neither Riddle nor Conway answered the rancorous response in a public fashion, but the fact that War Admiral appeared under colors only a week later for the Queens County Handicap at Aqueduct might indicate that the two men felt some urgency to oblige and appease. The Queens County offered a purse of less than five percent of the golden-paved trail of the match race, and at one mile perhaps was not the most logical of tests for a horse who had been primed for a mile and one-quarter. Three months had passed since the Widener. Nevertheless, War Admiral took up 132 pounds and gave six to Snark, fresh from his Suburban triumph. When word got around that War Admiral and Snark would be heading to the post, prospective rivals dropped out, all save for Danger Point (112) and Rudie (109).

The crowd was said to be 12,000, about half of the Suburban crowd and perhaps barely more than one-quarter of the number that would have overrun the turnstiles if the May 30 match had transpired. The 12,000 were ready with hisses and catcalls as War Admiral went to the post, presumably not out of malice for the swashbuckling little star himself, but in frustration and general displeasure with various two-legged forms that had been party of the goings-on of

recent weeks. Venting of spleens might have been gratifying, but a crowd of horseplayers is not wont to let
emotions block good-old monetary policy. The crowd
that booed also made War Admiral a strong favorite at
barely more than 1-2 as against Snark's odds of about
the reverse.

"As if conscious of the responsibility resting upon
him, this time the Admiral gave little trouble and broke
from his stall (No. 1) with facility," wrote Hervey. With
the weight conditions, however, Kurtsinger recognized
that, for once, darting pell-mell to set up a merry chase
was not the prudent move. Rudie was allowed to open
a lead of three lengths after a quarter-mile, and when
half of the race had been recorded at :46 1/5, War
Admiral was still only one length closer. He continued
his gradual ascent and came to within a length of the
leader after six furlongs in 1:11 2/5. Snark was four
lengths in arrears.

War Admiral swooped to command turning for
home, but, once again, he went wide while the challenger dashed along the rail. Jockey John Longden
brought Snark along the inside, but before he gained
a position beside the leader, War Admiral wandered

back over to the rail, forcing Snark to move outside to continue his bid. Snark's challenge was serious, but whereas Longden went to the whip, Kurtsinger merely rattled his own saber a bit, as he allowed War Admiral to drift back out slightly. War Admiral held off Snark to win by a length in 1:36 4/5, which was within four-fifths of a second of the stakes mark set by his sire's old foe John P. Grier seventeen years before. The Metropolitan Handicap winner, Danger Point (112), was third.

Nothing soothes the wronged horseplayer like a virtuoso performance by a great horse. The crowd voiced its approval at least as lustily as it had expelled its ungenerous frustrations only minutes before.

Ahead, though, lay another bit of a tease, followed by yet another disappointment, followed by an upset.

Three weeks later Suffolk Downs was ready for the fourth running of the rich, $50,000 Massachusetts Handicap. Seabiscuit had won the race the previous year, and it was made known that whatever malaise in training had befallen him and caused his withdrawal from the match race, he was back in percolating form and would defend his title. Riddle was ready for com-

bat as well, and so was War Admiral. It seemed that, after all the efforts for a special event, it was a regularly scheduled handicap that would give the public what it had longed to see for almost a year.

Seabiscuit's jockey, Red Pollard, suffered an excruciating leg fracture in a mishap while exercising a horse a few days before the Massachusetts Handicap. The great jockey George Woolf was called in to ride the Howard star, but rain through the final days before the race threatened Seabiscuit's participation. *American Race Horses of 1938* reported that Seabiscuit was scratched at "the last moment permissible" forty-five minutes before post time. Hillenbrand, in her diligent research, found the circumstances even more melodramatic. By her telling, Smith found heat in one of Seabiscuit's legs as he was preparing to take him to the paddock, and his rush to the stewards' stand to scratch the horse came after the statutory deadline. As the other runners were being assembled, veterinarians were called to Seabiscuit's barn, either to confirm Smith's judgment or to back up the stewards in their suspicion of a ruse. The veterinarians supported Smith's thought that the horse was injured, and the stewards relented.

Meantime, another crowd — this one said to number 70,000 — was sent into its turn of convulsive acrimony.

Riddle, ill again and accompanied to the races by his physician, had not been happy with the prospect of running War Admiral in the deep, wet footing. Whether out of sportsmanship, overriding confidence in his horse, a weariness borne of his illness, or a reluctance to subject himself to another round of boos, he had not scratched War Admiral.

Even without Seabiscuit, the Mass Cap of 1938 presented a tough task.

War Admiral and Seabiscuit had each been assigned 130 pounds. The Riddle colt thus was giving from twenty-three to twenty-nine pounds of actual weight to the five remaining runners. One of these, beneath 107 pounds, was the three-year-old Menow, who had been the champion two-year-old of the previous year. At three Hal Price Headley's Menow had been second to Bull Lea in the Blue Grass Stakes and fourth behind Lawrin in the Kentucky Derby. He had improved to third in Dauber's Preakness and then had won the Withers Stakes five weeks before the Massachusetts.

None other than Charley Kurtsinger had ridden Menow to victory in the previous year's Champagne and Futurity, and his determination to ride the colt in the Derby almost caused his undoing. At the time, Kurtsinger was riding first call for Mrs. Isabel Dodge Sloane's Brookmeade Stable. Hugh Fontaine was training the Brookmeade horses, and in the spring of 1938 he had told his rider not to travel from New York to Kentucky to ride Menow in an overnight handicap at Keeneland on April 15. Kurtsinger went ahead, and duly won the race on the Headley colt. Thereupon, Fontaine complained to the stewards in New York, and a flurry of reports had it that the rider would be suspended. It even was suggested that the suspension might be long enough to cost Kurtsinger the ride on War Admiral in the proposed May 30 match race against Seabiscuit. This was countered by explanation that stewards at Jamaica had no authority to extend suspensions for more than ten days after the meeting under their own jurisdiction ended, which was on May 7, but Riddle was said to have lined up jockey Wayne Wright in reserve, in case Kurtsinger was unable to ride War Admiral.

When matters were sorted out, it was explained further that Kurtsinger had made it back to New York the day after the Kentucky race to fulfill his commitment to Brookmeade as Jamaica opened on April 16. Moreover, by the end of April, the matter was resolved, and Kurtsinger clearly would be available for War Admiral, although it transpired that he did not return to Kentucky to ride Menow again. Al Robertson rode Menow in the Blue Grass, and then Sonny Workman was aboard in the Derby and Preakness.

Kurtsinger was reunited with Menow to win the Withers Stakes, but stuck to his old friend War Admiral for the Mass Cap. Nick Wall got the mount that day on Menow. War Admiral, having won his last eleven races, was sent off at 2-5, while Menow, despite his feathery weight and recent victory in the Withers, was allowed to slip away at 10-1. Going a mile and one-eighth in June, the scale called for a four-year-old to give a three-year-old twelve pounds. War Admiral was giving the young champion twenty-three pounds of actual weight, eleven by scale.

Many things had gone awry from the perfection that had seemed to beckon the meeting of two great

horses. That, plus the foreboding caste that rain and a heavy track always create at the races, could give one reason to suspect that what would happen on Mass Cap day was that Menow would scud away early, open a big lead, and gallop home while the long winning streak of the favorite came to a dismal conclusion. What was actually destined to happen that day was that Menow would scud away early, open a big lead, and gallop home while the long winning streak of the favorite came to a dismal conclusion.

Further to emphasize the gloominess from the vantage point of the Riddle stable, War Admiral, after struggling to get to second midway of the race, could not challenge and was even denied third, behind Menow and Busy K., by War Minstrel and the mocking lens of the photo-finish camera. He finished fourth, beaten eight lengths while unplaced for the first and only time in his career.

Had Seabiscuit been sound enough to run, he may or may not have been able to cope with Menow, and possibly War Admiral's star would have taken a more spectacular dip than it did.

Conway gave War Admiral a rest of several weeks,

pointing him next for the Saratoga meeting. At two and three, War Admiral had been forced by sickness or soundness troubles to miss the glamorous and clamorous meeting at the Spa, but at four he was finally able to participate. He lined up for the three-thousand-dollar Wilson Stakes on July 27, again dropping back to a mile. Conditions placed but 126 on his back, and only the three-year-old Fighting Fox (116) and the tough old mare Esposa (121) were entered against him. Esposa owned a renowned victory over Seabiscuit, having upset him by a nose in the previous year's Bowie Handicap. The vulnerability shown by War Admiral in the Mass Cap did not relegate him to any less than odds-on favoritism, at 3-5, but the short odds of 11-5 offered on Esposa illustrated the thought that the mare might snare another champion male.

Fighting Fox set the early pace, but Kurtsinger soon bid War Admiral take his accustomed position in front, and he did so without exertion. He quickly established daylight, and he increased his margin steadily until he hit the wire eight lengths before the full brother to his fellow Triple Crown winner, Gallant Fox. Fighting Fox had Esposa well measured

for second. The time was 1:39 2/5.

The Saratoga Handicap was one of the principal middle-distance races for older males at the Spa for many years, and three days after the Wilson, War Admiral came out again for that mile and one-quarter event. He was assigned top weight of 130 pounds for the $7,500 race, which had already been won by two of Man o' War's sons, Mars and Marine. Esposa again was sent against him, and as her prowess was canted toward the longer distances, it again was thought she might be a strong challenger. She was getting fourteen pounds this time, only a pound less than she had gotten from Seabiscuit in her victory over him the previous autumn. The three others in the Saratoga Handicap were receiving from eighteen to twenty-four pounds from War Admiral, who was priced at 7-10.

Esposa's breeder and owner, William Ziegler Jr., was reliving the trying times of the mare's sire, Espino, who in his colors had managed a successful career although being overshadowed by other sons of Man o' War, namely Crusader and Mars (not to mention another relative, the Fair Play colt Display).

Esposa chased the Admiral from the start, not allowing him to get more than a length or two ahead of her.
Storms had made the old track slow, which suited the
mare, and when jockey Wall got down to earnest urging, she came at War Admiral in the stretch. Riddle's
pronouncements about not letting the horse run under
excessive weights might have been instrumental in
War Admiral's having not been assigned much over
the testing standard of 130 pounds, and this might
well have been expected to be the last handicap of his
career. Nevertheless, Kurtsinger had been counseled
not to win by more than was prudent, and he resist-
ed the temptation to drive his colt in response to the
mare's challenge. Esposa was under the whip and gaining, but Kurtsinger's confidence was such that he hand
rode War Admiral, while allowing the mare to become
lapped on him. The official margin was a neck victory,
although some photos indicated the mare was beaten
by something more like three-quarters of a length. The
mile was reached in 1:39, and the final time was 2:06.

Three weeks passed before War Admiral's next
venture. True to the way horses for years were cam-
paigned at Saratoga, Esposa, on the other hand, had

run twice more in between, being unplaced in the Merchants' & Citizens' Handicap and then winning the Champlain. Yet again she lined up against War Admiral, for the weight-for-age Whitney Stakes at a mile and one-quarter. It was a replay of the Wilson cast, with Fighting Fox the only other character. At 126 pounds, War Admiral was sent off at 1-3. The scale placed 121 on the mare and 117 on the three-year-old.

Kurtsinger had been injured in a spill, and for the first time since War Admiral's third start at two, someone else was aboard. Breaking the streak of seventeen races was jockey Wayne Wright, who, it will be recalled, had been on standby were Kurtsinger to have been administratively deleted for the scheduled May 30 match.

Man o' War himself twice had new riders during his Saratoga soiree of 1920, Earl Sande and Andy Schuttinger being aboard for the Miller and the Travers respectively, and it had made no difference. Likewise, little War Admiral was apparently perfectly content with whatever altered nuance of stirrup and bit pressure he might have perceived. He was in front at every marker, and the pace was swift for the era and track, :23 3/5, :47 3/5, 1:12 3/5, 1:38. Wright had him under a bit of a hold most of the way on this joy ride, and when the doughty old Esposa put in her run, she "could not menace," in the jargon of the chart caller.

The final time was 2:03 4/5 as War Admiral held her safe by a length under mild urging.

Exactly a month after his first lifetime competitive appearance at Saratoga, War Admiral was fitted for his fourth. On August 27, closing day, his assignment was the longest of his career to that time, the mile and three-quarters Saratoga Cup. Once again, he was to carry 126 and, incredibly, owner Ziegler and trainer Matt Brady had Esposa ready for another tilt at their private windmill. For the third time, there was a three-horse field, it falling to the three-year-old Anaflame to fill in for stablemate Fighting Fox. Hervey later commented that "it is almost inexplicable that Esposa should have been at such short odds as 3-1, with the colt at 1-3 and Anaflame at 25-1...How was she going to beat The Admiral, who had just whipped her three times hand-running and was now essaying a distance all in his favor — well, it was a conundrum!"

Moose Peters, who had ridden War Admiral in the first race of his career, was aboard for the occasion, and he was well versed in the qualities of his mount. When the tape went up, Peters hustled War Admiral into the lead, and the colt soon reduced all questions to curiosity as to how his relative times would stack up to precedent. It was a display of machine-like efficiency with a touch of the inevitable. The quarters were reeled off at such pace that when War Admiral had completed a mile and a half, his time of 2:30 2/5 was more than a second faster than the track record for a race of that distance. A quarter-mile remained, and in its final stages, Peters was reining in War Admiral, who nonetheless won by four lengths over Esposa. The complete time of 2:55 4/5 suggested that, if pressed by another horse or scuffled along by his rider, War Admiral might well have reduced the track record of 2:55 set by Reigh Count and the American record of 2:54 3/5 set by Chilhowee.

"So faultless an exhibition was it of all the qualities which go to constitute the race horse of the highest class," rhapsodized Hervey, "that when he came prancing back to the stand, apparently unaffected by his effort, it rose to him and he was applauded to the echo."

WAR ADMIRAL

CHAPTER 7

The Admiral And The Biscuit

The interwoven theme of the year continued to be an echo of another sort — "Seabiscuit and War Admiral must meet, Seabiscuit and War Admiral must meet."

The Jockey Club Gold Cup on October 1 became the next vehicle of possibility for such a meeting. Seabiscuit had been eligible for the Saratoga Cup but had been in California on the day. Now, his Western summer campaign concluded, he would be again in the East, and both horses were named for the Gold Cup, which at two miles was then the longest major race run in America. On September 20, however, Seabiscuit was beaten in the Manhattan Handicap, a result that, in Hervey's phrase, "chilled any ardor that his stable might have held for an encounter over two miles with his younger rival." Seabiscuit repaired to Maryland and other targets.

War Admiral had only two rivals in the Gold Cup, which had been won by his sire in its second running in 1920. Both his brash opponents were three-year-olds, carrying 117 pounds by scale to the older horse's 124 pounds. One of them was Magic Hour, who the week before had won the longest major stakes for three-year-olds, the mile and five-eighths Lawrence Realization. Any suggestion that this made him a danger to War Admiral was apparently dismissed by the crowd, which sent the older colt off at 1-12. "Galloping" was the key chart conclusion after War Admiral, with Wright aboard again, toured in front throughout. "At no stage was he urged and was galloping along under restraint through the stretch."

War Admiral won by three lengths over Magic Hour, with Jolly Tar ten lengths farther back. The final time was 3:24 4/5, not spectacular but efficient. Riddle thus had won the race three times, with Man o' War and his sons Crusader and War Admiral. Riddle felt well enough to accept the latest of this trilogy of trophies in the winner's circle, perhaps taking smug pride in the accolades from a New York audience that had been disgruntled with him only months before.

Time was running short if the dream race were indeed to take place. Young Alfred Vanderbilt, the dashing, visionary sportsman who had agreed to take over operation of Pimlico, had been monitoring the situation all along. He knew he could not come close to a $100,000 purse, but he had some unusual cards in his own deck. For one, he had recently honeymooned with a niece of Mrs. Charles S. Howard, and so he had no trouble getting in touch with Seabiscuit's owner. Secondly, Vanderbilt as owner of the earlier handicap star Discovery had accepted as much as 143 pounds on his champion, so if he spoke of airy principles of sportsmanship he had plenty of moral clout to back up his position. Vanderbilt offered a purse of $15,000 and would convert his Pimlico Special into a match race at a mile and three-sixteenths. The distance, same as that of the Preakness, was more practical at Pimlico than the more common test of a mile and one quarter, which at his track would have dictated a start on the stretch turn.

Riddle had some problems with the way Pimlico's starter had put tongs on his colt while wrestling him to the starting gate in the past. So, he added one more wrinkle: New York's George Cassidy would be brought in to administer the start. Furthermore, fearing War Admiral's tendency toward antics in the new starting gates, he insisted on a walk-up start. Howard took the tack that it was necessary to concede such matters, and he and Riddle also agreed on the weight of 120 pounds each.

Finally, the race was set. Vanderbilt recognized that a weekend crowd would be so immense that his track could not serve them very well, sending thousands home with a poor impression of what going racing was all about, so he opted for a weekday, Tuesday, November 1. The date was a full month after War Admiral's Gold Cup and a bit more than two weeks since Seabiscuit (under 126 pounds) was upset by the lightly weighted filly Jacola (102) in the Laurel Handicap.

War Admiral was thus coming into the race off four consecutive victories and had won sixteen of his past seventeen races. Seabiscuit's run up to the race could be cast in whatever light appealed to the opinion of the individual: one win in his past three races, or three wins in his past five, five of his past eight, but also five of his past eleven.

Given the last-hour and last-quarter-hour dramas

of earlier proposed meetings, it was no certainty that the race would actually take place until the horses approached the start late that afternoon. In fact, both owners had placed upon Maryland Racing Commission chairman Jervis Spencer the responsibility of walking the track that morning and determining whether it figured to be a fast track that afternoon. Had Spencer shaken his head on the matter, the race might yet again have been scuttled. Conway, however, had not waited for a perfect track for War Admiral's final work, having sent him the race distance in 2:02 over a sloppy track on October 28.

Finally, all the stars aligned. The race actually would take place, with race caller Clem McCarthy stationed to give a national radio audience a memorable call — obstructed vision notwithstanding. Weekday or not, the crowd of 40,000 exceeded Pimlico's seating capacity by about 24,000 on a lovely Indian summer afternoon.

In the *Daily Mirror*, columnist Fred Keats was among the writers eager finally to pick up on the theme from the spring as to what would happen: "Liking for Pimlico in Biscuit's Favor" was the headline over the article in which Keats commented, "...the famous match should

result in a far better contest than the $100,000 Belmont Park event would have been. Seabiscuit now is ready to run his best race and as War Admiral always is fit, there should be no excuses from either side...Sentiment sways the players more than it does the bookmakers and the players are on the side of War Admiral for the very good reason that he has seldom failed them. Seabiscuit also is consistent. He never runs a real bad race, but he does not win with that monotonous regularity that has made War Admiral a public idol. It is true that some of Seabiscuit's defeats were better performances than some of War Admiral's victories, but the average player does not go into the matter that deeply."

Match races have a long, but diminishing history in American racing. In previous centuries, such two-horse events as American Eclipse-Henry (1823), Fashion-Boston (1842), Lexington-Lecompte (1855), Ten Broeck-Mollie McCarthy (1878), and Domino-Henry of Navarre (1894) had an air of exhilarating purity. In more recent times, match races had attempted to bring together the best from Europe and their American counterparts, as exemplified by the 1923 Zev-Papyrus match, while Myrtlewood-Clang

(1935) matched sprinters.

At the time of the long-awaited Seabiscuit-War Admiral match, the concept of a two-horse race perhaps still had some of the image of the purest contest. Howard, at least, had long wanted such a race as opposed to having them meet in a "field," carrying the notion that it was a truer test. In fact, however, horse racing as it has evolved is more complicated than an equine *mano a mano*. The qualities required to become a great and consistent winner the way racing is regularly conducted have to do with responding to pace and traffic and weights and distance. The skill and mind-set of being a great horse amenable to various strategies go beyond bursting out to try to wear down a single opponent.

When racing as a whole was match racing, then the best horse at match racing could be counted the champion. Once the sport evolved into a pattern of larger fields, the exercise became more complicated.

Still, in 1938, the perceived purity of a match retained some of its charm. George Woolf, who was to ride Seabiscuit, discerned, however, that no matter what a horse's general strategy was in a regular race, it was

imperative to go out early in a match and take the race to a singular opponent. No matter how much you might use your horse early, if he subdued the rival, he had it won, with no worry about a lesser horse coming along to pass exhausted duelists. Woolf was not alone in that recognition. The United Press' Henry McLemore commented in an article published on the day of the race, "The chances are (Seabiscuit) will try to match strides with his rival from the start and see how the 'mighty mite' reacts when he is unable to put daylight between himself and a challenger. Seabiscuit normally is a slow starter, reserving his move for the late stages of the race. But hanging back is considered fatal in a two-horse race."

Since 1938 there have been some few superb two-horse contests — Alsab over Whirlaway (1942) and Convenience over Typecast (1972) come to mind. By and large, though, match races in years after the Seabiscuit-War Admiral meeting have had a history of disappointment, or worse. The most ballyhooed of match races have been sullied by another of the truths: If only two horses are entered, and the world holds its breath, it is very difficult for the owner of either contestant to withdraw. The Assault-Armed match of the

123

1940s was lessened by widespread word that Assault was not at his best, and then in the next decade the Nashua-Swaps spectacle was besmirched in many minds by the belief that Swaps was unsound. Then, in 1975, the worst of all results found the heroine Ruffian fatally injured in her match with the colt Foolish Pleasure.

The 1938 Pimlico Special was a marker along the way to the demise of the match race as a form recognized as conclusive for the best American horses. To suggest that there was something other than a true race that day, however, would be unfair to Seabiscuit. As the late Kent Hollingsworth summarized years later in *The Great Ones*, "All things considered, War Admiral was better than Seabiscuit, but he was not that day..." While it was the widespread notion that War Admiral, whose many great moments had been dictated from the front, would take the lead at the start, it was Woolf on the later running Seabiscuit who gunned to the lead. What a demanding race he made of it. With Kurtsinger at last back aboard, War Admiral chased, War Admiral closed gamely, War Admiral struggled, War Admiral fell away. Seabiscuit turned back the Triple Crown winner's grim challenge and drew off to

win by four lengths in 1:56 3/5. This broke the Pimlico record that had been set that spring by none other than War Admiral's old rival Pompoon. The winner was sent off at 2.20-1, War Admiral at 1-4.

Hillenbrand quoted winning rider Woolf as having walked the track and found a path that was made firmer by tractors passing over it, but was obscured by harrow marks. He said he told himself to get to that path early and follow it around the track.

"I have no excuse," Kurtsinger said soon after the race. "War Admiral simply didn't have it today...The Admiral came to him and looked him in the eye, but that other horse refused to quit. We gave all we had. It just wasn't good enough."

Hillenbrand quoted Woolf, "I saw something in the Admiral's eyes that was pitiful. He looked all broken up. I don't think he will be good for another race. Horses, mister, can have crushed hearts just like humans."

Seabiscuit's climb to the mountain top was complete. He would be the Horse of the Year for 1938.

In an apparent effort to lend conclusiveness to the event, some of the most distinguished writers took shots at War Admiral, likening the horse to some sort of pampered rich kid who had things handed to him.

Stunningly, as renowned a sportswriter as Grantland Rice diminished himself with a diatribe that, "The Admiral had known only the softer years — the softer type of competition...he had run against too many plow horses and platers in his soft, easy life. He had never tackled a Seabiscuit before." Yeah, a Triple Crown and a sequence of handicap races usually are looked upon as "soft" going for a racehorse. Seabiscuit presumably was the best horse War Admiral had faced, but Riddle's horse had hardly made his reputation by taking on bums.

Bob Considine, an adroit sports writer before going on to distinction as a general and wartime correspondent and broadcast host, had more fittingly addressed War Admiral's courage quotient after the previous year's Belmont:

"Bleeding from a great gash in his right front leg, split at the very start of the race, War Admiral, the courageous son of Man o' War, was crowned with the wreath of racing immortality at Belmont Park today... there was no quit in him. He was behind (briefly) and

it infuriated him. With one enormous punch at the perfect loam of the track, War Admiral shoved those eager nostrils into the cool dustless air that is sucked in only by the leaders. He came up and looked Flying Scot in the eye and then burst past."

Woolf's dire prognosis of a broken equine heart notwithstanding, Conway and Riddle soldiered on with War Admiral, hoping for another meeting with Seabiscuit. Eleven days after the Pimlico Special, War Admiral was back under colors in New England, where Narragansett Park offered the $10,000-added Rhode Island Handicap. Seabiscuit was also eligible, and the weights were not announced until three days before the event. In keeping with his new status as established king of the hill, Seabiscuit was assigned 130 pounds to War Admiral's 127. Track management made it known that the purse would be upped to $25,000 if both ran, but Howard decided to keep Seabiscuit in Maryland. He would not race again that year, and why should he?

War Admiral was installed a 1-20 choice at a track where he had never before appeared. Such confidence on the part of the public is compelling considering that he was coming off a decisive defeat and was facing a tricky task. War Admiral was giving twelve pounds to the accomplished handicapper Mucho Gusto, winner of eight races during the year, and fifteen pounds to Busy K., who had finished ahead of War Admiral in the Riddle colt's last, dismal venture into New England. The three others carried weights down to as little as 101 pounds.

War Admiral was drawn on the outside of a six-horse field, but resorted to his hard-headed tactics. Perhaps he was never comfortable being in a stall with nothing else to his right. At any rate, he once again was taken outside the gate and then broke alertly. Mucho Gusto took the lead, and Kurtsinger allowed his little champion to track the latter into the backstretch. There, he let out a notch and War Admiral ran up to and past the other horse, opening as much as a six-length lead as they turned for home. His heart and legs and mind were apparently all still intact, as he rambled through the stretch, Kurtsinger taking him up sufficiently in the final furlong for Mucho Gusto to climb back up to within two and a half lengths of him. Busy K. was third. The time of 1:51 2/5 for the mile and one-eighth was two seconds over Stagehand's track record.

War Admiral thus had won nine of eleven races at four to earn $90,840. His combined record at three and four was seventeen wins from nineteen starts.

(Horse of the Year Seabiscuit had earned considerably more, $130,395, having won six of eleven that year. The leading owner was Maxwell Howard — not a relative of Seabiscuit's owner — whose Stagehand had defeated Seabiscuit in the Santa Anita Handicap. Stagehand also had won the Santa Anita Derby and then several major Eastern handicaps.)

Conway took War Admiral back to Glen Riddle in Berlin, where his assignment was to rest him and then prepare him for a second sojourn to Florida for the Widener. When Hialeah's impresario devised the race, he stipulated that the Challenge Cup would pass to the possession of the owner of a horse that could win the race a second time. That stipulation, the purse, and the prestige appealed to Riddle, and he looked toward the race as an appealing farewell before War Admiral was sent into the stud at Faraway Farm.

Although he had issued no excuses in the immediate aftermath of the Pimlico Special, Kurtsinger had begun to recant his position. By December he was expressing confidence and yearning for a rematch. "I'm just hoping we get another crack at him this winter," Kurtsinger was quoted in the *Daily Racing Form*, "possibly in the Widener Handicap. He's (Seabiscuit) a tough horse; yes, a great horse but I still believe we can beat him..."

Moreover, Kurtsinger had convinced himself — or said he had, anyway — that "The Admiral wasn't himself that day (Pimlico Special). The tip-off came in the first quarter. Although I had a steadying hold, you know he should have stepped it" through the first half mile "in better than :47 2/5. Look at his Derby, and other races. Too much Cup racing, I guess."

This last comment alluded to the fact that the horse's two previous races had been at one and three-quarters miles and two miles, and suggested that War Admiral's speed might have been dulled a bit — a common handicapping observation when horses shorten from one race to another. (The comment might be construed as critical of Conway for failing to give the horse enough speed work or a prep race to sharpen him for the shorter distance.) The description of a type of event as "Cup" races reflected traditional nomenclature of that time.

While a race of any distance might be called a "Cup," of course, there had grown a tendency to describe as "Cup races" and "Cup horses" the echelon embracing the longest distance tests, such as the Saratoga Cup, Pimlico Cup, and Jockey Club Gold Cup. This imitated English racing custom. While "Cup races" in that sense have virtually disappeared in America, England even to this day has a relatively strong sequence of "Cup races" at two miles or more, such as the Goodwood Cup, Ascot Gold Cup, etc.

Kurtsinger's comments were published on December 11. About a month later, Riddle announced that he was taking The Flying Dutchman off War Admiral!

Kurtsinger, stung, announced his retirement. (This first retirement was brief. He came back in the spring, having modest success in riding twenty-six winners that year. At the end of 1939, Kurtsinger's career record was 721 [thirteen percent] wins from 5,651 mounts, with earnings of $1,729,785. He announced plans to come back again a time or two, but injuries and then illness precluded it. He died of complications from pneumonia at thirty-nine in 1946. Kurtsinger was elected to the National Museum of

Racing's Hall of Fame in 1967.)

Many years later, in 1961, the *New York Herald-Tribune* published a column recalling that immediately after the match race, Riddle had "bawled imprecations in the clubhouse (while) Kurtsinger sat bawling quietly in the attic room where the jockeys dressed. That night Charley caught a train for Louisville in a state of deep depression.

"He was pretty sure he had lost the mount as well as the race, for he knew Sam Riddle's reputation. The old man had never ceased blackguarding Johnny Loftus for the only defeat of Man o' War's life back in 1919."

Caution is needed in attempting to sift through conflicting stories. Riddle might well have become convinced that Loftus had ridden poorly in the 1919 Sanford Memorial, undoubtedly having it said to him many times over the years by fans declaring that Man o' War "should have" been undefeated. However, at the time, he had retained Loftus as Man o' War's jockey for his remaining three races at two, and, more tellingly, after Loftus' license was denied, Riddle went personally to a meeting of The Jockey Club stewards to request the rider's reinstatement.

As for whether the owner was incensed immediately after the 1938 Pimlico Special and the rider convinced he had lost the mount, it need be remembered that Kurtsinger's optimistic comments about a second meeting with Seabiscuit were published more than a month after the race!

At whatever point and for whatever reasons Riddle came to his decision, by January 9 the change had been made public and Wayne Wright was to ride War Admiral when he made his debut at five on February 18, 1939. The horse was under 126 pounds in an overnight race at seven furlongs. At such distance were two proven stayers facing one another, for the race also drew the 1938 Belmont Stakes winner, Pasteurized, in at 119 pounds. War Admiral, however, was favored at 1-5. He broke from the second stall from the rail and dominated, taking a length and a half lead early and won by a half-length under a mild hand ride.

The Widener was set for March 4, and War Admiral was given top weight of 131 pounds. Seabiscuit was nursing an injury on the West Coast and would not start for a year. A few days before the Widener, War Admiral was reported to have a temperature and had to be declared. Riddle's stance on weights and conditions, and his scratching of the horse from the previous year's Suburban, had engendered in the press some underlying cynicism. It seems odd that the owner of a War Admiral would be accused of being timid about facing challenges, especially since he had let his colt face Seabiscuit on a Pimlico track on which he had struggled before. Nevertheless, it was suggested in a few columns that the owner wanted an excuse not to face Stagehand, who had set a track record in winning the McLennan at Hialeah on the same day War Admiral won his prep. War Admiral once again was returned to Glen Riddle in Maryland.

Riddle changed his mind about standing the horse at stud that season and allowed Conway to ship him north with the thought of further racing. It was announced, however, that he would run only on courses favorable to him, and so one of the big Eastern races to be missed was the Dixie Handicap at Pimlico, scene of some of his tougher victories and most resounding defeat.

The long, mostly cheerful voyage of War Admiral, Riddle, Conway, et al., was nearing its conclusion, and one part of that reality was sad, indeed. Conway's

health had been failing, and the stable's shipment on to the northern tracks was delayed by his illness, as assistant Joe Farrell was briefly in charge. The Riddle stable and Conway later went north, and, again, there was an announced change of plans. War Admiral was scheduled to go on to Suffolk Downs to aim for the Massachusetts Handicap, despite his poor experience in the race the previous year. The colt was supposedly in training, but he had not started since his lone appearance at Hialeah in mid-February.

The stable was still in New York when on May 13, a publication named *Collyer's Eye* reported that War Admiral had broken down and would soon be retired. On May 24, *Daily Racing Form* followed with a report based "on reliable information" that War Admiral had wrenched an ankle and was out of serious training, and the next day the publication added that he was unwinding for his retirement to stud. It was not until several more weeks had passed, however, that Riddle on June 15 made the announcement verifying the horse's retirement. A breeding season thus had been relinquished and the only compensation was the allowance victory.

In the meantime, Conway had suffered what was described as "a physical breakdown" at his barn at Belmont Park. On May 22, on the advice of his doctors, he announced his retirement from training. A lifelong bachelor, Conway returned to Oceanport, New Jersey, from whence his career had begun. On June 19, less than a month after his retirement and as his great ward was returning to Kentucky, the trainer of War Admiral died at the home of his sister, Ella Conway.

Faraway Farm had dispatched an employee, Bob Hurst, to New York to accompany War Admiral back to Faraway, and they arrived at the Southern Railway Company's Lexington station at 9:45 on the morning of June 20 — the same day reports of Conway's death were published. The champion was photographed by reporters there and then vanned to the farm. War Admiral had run twenty-six times, won twenty-one, finished second three times and third once, and was unplaced only in the Massachusetts Handicap. He earned $273,240. He had convinced Conway that he was "faster than Crusader" and the greatest of Man o' War's sons.

H.I. Phillips penned a pleasingly sentimental poem, entitled "A Trainer Passes":

The Admiral comes slowly up the road,
Upon the farm so green where he was born;
He halts as if he'd heard a bugle blow...
What is it that he seems to sense this morn?

He pauses, taut, with every nerve alert,
In that strange way that a thoroughbred will do
Perceiving something in the distant hills,
And seeing something in the far-off blue

Something has happened; now the Admiral
Is conscious of it as he paws the ground...
He searches forms and faces in the group
And knows that one he knew is not around.

He goes into his stall, his head now low;
No more will bugles call him to the post...
But hark! He hears one blowing from afar;
It calls the trainer that he loved the most.

CHAPTER 8

A Lasting Legacy

Man o' War was a great sire of racehorses and daughters that produced them, and he got a few sons who carried on well in the stud. Of Riddle's early stars by the great champion, American Flag begot sixteen stakes winners (a solid nine percent) including the champion filly Nellie Flag. Crusader, on the other hand, made less of a mark at stud, getting a half-dozen stakes winners (five percent).

Given the weakness in War Admiral's female family, it could hardly be said he took to the stud the entire package of pedigree to match his high class as a runner, but he was, after all, a champion son of Man o' War, and he would be given his chance. He even had one advantage Man o' War had not enjoyed: Riddle pursued a more open policy in accepting outside owners' mares.

War Admiral's first crop included four stakes winners, of which the filly Bee Mac won the Hopeful Stakes and Spinaway. Bee Mac was bred by Colonel E.R. Bradley, who had an immediate interest in breeding to War Admiral and had five seasons a year to him. Although it could not be recognized at the time, of course, War Admiral's first crop also set into motion the stallion's long-lasting influence as a broodmare sire, for it included Iron Maiden, destined to be the dam of one Kentucky Derby winner (Iron Liege) and the second dam of another (Swaps)!

In War Admiral's second crop came the great filly Busher, who was bred by Colonel Bradley and later raced by Hollywood mogul Louis B. Mayer. Busher had the audacity at three to defeat the older male champion Armed, and in 1945 she followed her immediate predecessor, Twilight Tear, as the second (and still last) three-year-old filly to be named Horse of the Year. War Admiral ascended to the top of the American sire list that year, although his oldest horses were only four. His progeny for the season earned $591,352, a single-year record for any stallion to that time.

In his crop of 1946, War Admiral sired the champion two-year-old of 1948, Blue Peter, as well as the second-rated colt, Mr. Busher, and led the juvenile sire list with $346,260. In the next crop came two fillies (both bred by Ogden Phipps) who starred on the racetrack and would be instrumental in extending War Admiral's influence into later decades. These were Busanda and Striking. Phipps had been another major breeder who sought War Admiral, and even before he took part in a three-way division of Colonel Bradley's elite Idle Hour Stock, Phipps had bought into the latter's La Troienne family through the acquisition of Big Hurry. Big Hurry's foals were to be instrumental in a barrage of important horses for Phipps and other breeders, including the champion Easy Goer and the top race mare and major producer Searching. Also a daughter of War Admiral, Searching was acquired by the Bieber-Jacobs Stable and became a mainstay of that prominent breeding operation as well as a lasting influence in her own right.

Striking was by War Admiral and out of another daughter of La Troienne, Baby League, and thus was a full sister to Busher. Striking won the Schuylerville Stakes for Phipps before launching her chapter of the broodmare production that would lead eventually

to Numbered Account and many other good horses. Busanda was by War Admiral and out of another daughter of La Troienne, Businesslike. Busanda won the Alabama and defeated males in the Suburban Handicap and two runnings of the Saratoga Cup. She then began her own important broodmare career distinguished by her foaling the great horse and lasting influence Buckpasser.

War Admiral sired a total of forty stakes winners (eleven percent) from 371 foals. The others included Admiral Vee, Blue Banner, Cold Command, Great Captain, War Command, and War Jeep.

In 1962, three years after his death, War Admiral's daughters produced earners of $1,654,396 to make him the leading broodmare sire. Thus, the Triple Crown winner on the racetrack had accomplished a hat trick, or another "Triple Crown" as it were, as a progenitor — leading sire, leading juvenile sire, and leading broodmare sire. He repeated as leading broodmare sire in 1964, when his total was $2,028,459. Once again, this was a single-season record. Also in 1964, War Admiral's daughters were represented by winners of 351 races, the most for any broodmare sire that year.

None of War Admiral's best racing sons went on to great success at stud, but his daughters foaled horses that were not only distinguished runners but important breeding animals, too. One of the grandsons was Buckpasser, a high-class sire whose continuing influence today also leans toward the produce of his daughters. The Jockey Club records show that 163 daughters of War Admiral produced 1,287 registered foals. Those 1,287 included 113 stakes winners, of which eight were champions. In addition to Buckpasser and Iron Liege, some of the others from his daughters were Affectionately, Hoist the Flag, Crafty Admiral, and Gun Bow. Crafty Admiral became the broodmare sire of Affirmed, while Striking was the second dam of Seattle Slew's broodmare sire. Thus, there would be a bit of the genetics of the fourth Triple Crown winner in the pedigrees of the tenth and eleventh.

(Insofar as the sire line of Man o' War, it fell to another of his later sons, War Relic, to generate the highest degree of lasting strength. The irascible War Relic, a Riddle homebred of 1938, had a notable victory over Whirlaway in the Narragansett Special. War Relic sired Intent, in turn the sire of Intentionally. It was to be

Intentionally's son, In Reality, who continued as one of the key links of Man o' War's sire line to the present, he siring Relaunch, Believe It, Known Fact, Valid Appeal, etc. Bringing this line up to date, in 2001 its representatives included two-time Breeders' Cup Classic winner Tiznow and the dazzling juvenile Officer.)

Samuel D. Riddle died in 1951, but it was not until 1958 that the executors of his estate sold his portion of Faraway Farm. War Admiral was by then a twenty-four-year-old stallion, and he was in need of a new home. Preston Madden was among several Kentucky farm owners interested in taking the proven leading sire, along with War Relic and two other Riddle stallions, Big Money and Somali II.

Madden was the young master of historic Hamburg Place outside Lexington. His grandfather, the legendary John E. Madden, had bred five Kentucky Derby winners on the farm, but Preston, himself, was unproven as a horseman and manager.

"I called the executors. They had the reputation of being tough, but they were extremely nice to me," Madden recalled late in 2001, more than forty years later. "Others had figured out that the stallions would be under new management, but I wanted them — the two best living sons of Man o' War — so I persevered. Other farms that wanted them were more renowned at that time, and the executors were hustled pretty hard, but I decided I would do everything in my power.

"I told them to tell me what they wanted, and I was pretty sure I could handle it. They were nice enough to say they didn't want to take advantage of me and they wanted suggestions from me. I agreed to pay all expenses, including a certain amount of advertising. The stud fees were sent to them (the Riddle Memorial Hospital in Media, Pennsylvania, was ultimate benefi- ciary). I took nothing but had the privilege of breeding three mares to each of the stallions."

Despite the recollection of the competition for the prestige of standing the horses, Madden also recalled that because of their ages, it was not easy to attract mares for War Admiral and War Relic. War Admiral was bred to thirteen mares in 1959.

The executors apparently never had reason to sec- ond-guess themselves. In 1964 Robert B. Greer of the law firm of Butler, Beatty, Greer, and Johnson wrote Madden: "I am glad we can thank War Relic for another

$1,000. War Relic should be grateful to you and Anita and your superintendent for softening his character and reputation, so that in his later years he would be known as a reasonably gentle horse...among the things which I shall always be glad and proud of is the fact that I had a small part in seeing that the Riddle stallions would be safely provided for without regard to their current abilities. Your stewardship is drawing to a close. You have been faithful beyond the call of duty..."

(Madden's other productive moves as a horseman included the purchase of T. V. Lark, who not only won the Washington, D.C., International over Kelso and other important races, but also gave Hamburg Place a leading sire that stood his entire career at the farm. T. V. Lark topped the general sire list in 1974.)

The last foal of War Admiral bred by Madden was Belthazar, a filly born in the spring of 1960. Belthazar was to become the second dam of Alysheba, a Madden-bred who was sold to the Clarence Scharbauer family for $500,000 at Keeneland. In 1987 Alysheba, descendant of War Admiral, fulfilled Preston Madden's abiding ambition to breed a sixth Kentucky Derby winner in the history of Hamburg Place.

EPILOGUE

The Old Champion

An eerie light bathed the scene as Preston Madden peered into War Admiral's stall at Hamburg Place. It was the last time the young man would see the old champion alive, although he did not know it at the time. As Madden thinks back to that evening in 1959, it is with a lasting sense of gratitude to the horse. For a young man making his own way in the business and sport of his grandfather, the acquisition of the greatest son of Man o' War was a boost in prestige and recognition, even if he had only been able to stand the horse one season.

"I was doing my active duty in the Army and had to get back to Fort Knox," Madden recalled of that night. "The horse had been sore in all four feet when we brought him over from Faraway Farm. Dr. Robert Bardwell did a great deal of help using Carotene (then

146

a popular stimulant to hoof growth). He really was a believer in Carotene."

Further comfort was provided by the heat lamp, which caused the eerie glow in the stall.

Still, the old Triple Crown winner's time was approaching.

"He was such a baby," Madden's wife, Anita, recalled. "He would shape the straw the same way in the middle of the stall every night and lie down."

War Admiral injured himself in the night and, at the age of twenty-five and in discomfort, there was no question but that he should be euthanized. Mrs. Madden had the unpleasant task of apprising Preston of that bad news after he had returned to Fort Knox.

"I asked to get some time off," Madden continued. "I needed to get back and take care of things like letting people who had booked mares to the horse for the next spring know what had happened. They said, 'Well, you're not going.' "

In 2001 the Maddens could not help but laugh at the memory of the brass shown by the young Anita. "She contacted the Red Cross to help us," Madden said. "Boy, was my company commander mad!"

War Admiral's death came on October 30, 1959. He was buried near the grave of his sire, in the shadow of the heroic-sized bronze of Man o' War executed by Herbert Haseltine. In 1976 the bronze and the attendant graves were removed from their little park on part of the old Faraway to the new Kentucky State Horse Park.

More than sixty years after their meeting, Seabiscuit and War Admiral would once again engage the public's sporting interest — thanks to the remarkable bestseller by Laura Hillenbrand. By then, the score between the two stood as:

• Winning races in head-to-head competition: Seabiscuit 1, War Admiral 0.

• Bestselling books about them: Seabiscuit 1, War Admiral 0.

• Hollywood movies about them: Seabiscuit 1 (soon to be 2), War Admiral 0.

As the twentieth century brought its spate of backward looks, though, War Admiral got in a win. *The Blood-Horse* assembled a panel of seven racing experts and historians to evaluate 100 years worth of champion American Thoroughbreds. War Admiral was ranked

thirteenth best of them all. Seabiscuit was ranked twenty-fifth, also a noble placement.

Both still deserve to be "applauded to the echo."

WAR ADMIRAL's
PEDIGREE

MAN O' WAR, ch, 1917	Fair Play, 1905	Hastings, 1893	Spendthrift / Cinderella
		Fairy Gold, 1896	Bend Or / Dame Masham
	Mahubah, 1910	Rock Sand, 1900	Sainfoin / Roquebrune
WAR ADMIRAL, brown colt, 1934		Merry Token, 1891	Merry Hampton / Mizpah
	Sweep, 1907	Ben Brush, 1893	Bramble / Roseville
		Pink Domino, 1897	Domino / Belle Rose
BRUSHUP, b, 1929	Annette K., 1921	Harry of Hereford, 1910	John o' Gaunt / Canterbury Pilgrim
		Bathing Girl, 1915	Spearmint / Summer Girl

WAR ADMIRAL's RACE RECORD

War Admiral — **br. c. 1934, by Man o' War (Fair Play)–Brushup, by Sweep** — **Lifetime record: 26 21 3 1 $273,240**

Own.– Glen Riddle Farm Stable
Br.– Samuel D. Riddle (Ky)
Tr.– G. Conway

18Feb39-6Hia	fst	7f	$:23^{3}$ $:46^{4}$ $1:10^{4}$ $1:22^{4}$	4↑	Alw 1500	2	1	$1^{1\frac{1}{2}}$	$1^{1\frac{1}{2}}$	$1^{\frac{1}{2}}$	$1^{\frac{1}{2}}$	Wright WD	126	w	*.20	99-05	WarAdmrl$126^{\frac{1}{2}}$Psturzd119^{12}SndyBoot110	Mild hand ride late	3
12Nov38-5Nar	fst	1⅛	$:47^{2}$ $1:11^{3}$ $1:37^{2}$ $1:51^{2}$	3↑	Rhode Island H 11k	6	2	1^{nk}	$1^{2\frac{1}{2}}$	1^{6}	$1^{2\frac{1}{2}}$	Kurtsinger C	127	w	*.20	91-17	War Admiral$127^{2\frac{1}{2}}$Mucho Gusto115^{1}Busy K.112no	Eased up	6
1Nov38-6Pim	fst	$1\frac{3}{16}$	$:47^{3}$ $1:11^{4}$ $1:36^{4}$ $1:56^{3}$	3↑	Pim Spl 15k	1	2	2^{1}	2no	$2^{\frac{1}{2}}$	2^{4}	Kurtsinger C	120	w	*.25	97-08	Seabiscuit120^{4}War Admiral120	No excuse	2
1Oct38-5Bel	fst	2	$:52^{2}$ $2:34^{3}$ $2:59^{1}$ $3:24^{4}$	3↑	J C Gold Cup 7k	2	1	$1^{1\frac{1}{2}}$	1^{2}	1^{2}	1^{3}	Wright WD	124	w	*.08	85-12	War Admiral124^{3}Magic Hour117^{10}Jolly Tar117^{3}	Galloping	3
	Geldings not eligible																		
27Aug38-5Sar	fst	1¾	$:48^{4}$ $2:05^{1}$ $2:30^{2}$ $2:55^{4}$	3↑	Sar Cup 8.3k	3	1	$1^{1\frac{1}{2}}$	$1^{1\frac{1}{2}}$	$1^{1\frac{1}{2}}$	1^{4}	Peters M	126	w	*.33	96-08	War Admiral126^{4}Esposa121^{10}Anaflame111	Easily	3
20Aug38-5Sar	fst	1¼	$:47^{3}$ $1:12^{3}$ $1:38$ $2:03^{4}$	3↑	Whitney 3.7k	3	1	1^{3}	1^{2}	1^{1}	1^{1}	Wright WD	126	w	*.33	90-11	War Admiral126^{1}Esposa121^{10}Fighting Fox117	Handily	3
	Geldings not eligible																		
30Jly38-5Sar	sl	1¼	$:49^{1}$ $1:14$ $1:39$ $2:06$	3↑	Saratoga H 10k	5	1	1^{2}	1^{1}	1^{2}	1^{nk}	Kurtsinger C	130	w	*.70	79-16	War Admiral130^{nk}Esposa116^{5}Isolater105.5^{4}	Under drive	5
27Jly38-5Sar	my	1	$:24$ $:48^{1}$ $1:13$ $1:39^{2}$	3↑	Wilson 3.9k	3	2	$1^{\frac{1}{2}}$	$1^{1\frac{1}{2}}$	1^{3}	1^{8}	Kurtsinger C	126	w	*.60	84-19	War Admiral126^{8}Fighting Fox$116^{1\frac{1}{2}}$Esposa121	Much best	3
	Geldings not eligible																		
29Jun38-6Suf	hy	1⅛	$:48^{1}$ $1:13^{2}$ $1:39^{3}$ $1:52^{3}$	3↑	Mass H 59k	6	4	$3^{2\frac{1}{2}}$	2^{4}	3^{3}	$4^{8\frac{1}{4}}$	Kurtsinger C	130	w	*.40	74-28	Menow107^{8}Busy K.107^{nk}War Minstrel106^{no}	Weakened	6
6Jun38-5Aqu	fst	1	$:23$ $:46^{1}$ $1:11^{2}$ $1:36^{4}$	3↑	Queens County H 6.1k	1	2	2^{2}	2^{1}	$1^{1\frac{1}{2}}$	1^{1}	Kurtsinger C	132	w	*.55	96-14	War Admiral132^{1}Snark126^{7}Danger Point$112^{1\frac{1}{2}}$	Driving	4
5Mar38-6Hia	fst	1¼	$:47^{1}$ $1:11^{3}$ $1:37$ $2:03^{4}$	3↑	Widener H 63k	13	3	1^{1}	1^{3}	1^{5}	$1^{1\frac{1}{2}}$	Kurtsinger C	130	w	*.35	90-12	War Admiral$130^{1\frac{1}{2}}$Zevson$104^{\frac{1}{2}}$War Minstrel111^{1}	Eased up	13
19Feb38-5Hia	fst	7f	$:23$ $:45^{2}$ $1:10^{1}$ $1:23^{4}$	4↑	Alw 1100	6	3	2^{nk}	$1^{1\frac{1}{2}}$	1^{4}	$1^{1\frac{1}{2}}$	Kurtsinger C	122		*.30	94-13	WarAdmiral$122^{1\frac{1}{2}}$SirOracle116^{6}CaballeroII$110^{2\frac{1}{2}}$	Eased up	6
3Nov37-5Pim	fst	$1\frac{3}{16}$	$:46^{2}$ $1:11^{2}$ $1:38$ $1:58^{4}$		Pim Spl H 8.2k	1	2	3^{1}	$2^{1\frac{1}{2}}$	1^{2}	$1^{1\frac{1}{2}}$	Kurtsinger C	128	w	*.05	96-13	WarAdmrl$128^{1\frac{1}{2}}$MaskedGenrl100^{4}WrMnstrl109^{no}	Won driving	4
30Oct37-5Lrl	gd	1¼	$:48$ $1:13$ $1:38^{4}$ $2:04^{4}$	3↑	Washington H 19k	7	3	1^{1}	1^{3}	$1^{1\frac{1}{2}}$	$1^{1\frac{1}{2}}$	Kurtsinger C	126	w	*.65	86-22	War Admiral$126^{1\frac{1}{2}}$Heelfly119^{2}Burning Star118^{3}	Easily	7
26Oct37-5Lrl	fst	$1\frac{1}{16}$	$:24^{1}$ $:48$ $1:13^{1}$ $1:46$	3↑	Alw 1200	8	1	1^{3}	1^{3}	1^{4}	$1^{2\frac{1}{2}}$	Kurtsinger C	106	w	*.40	87-21	War Admiral$106^{2\frac{1}{2}}$Aneroid113^{4}Floradora107^{hd}	Easily	8
5Jun37-5Bel	fst	1½	$:48$ $1:12^{1}$ $2:02^{1}$ $2:28^{3}$		Belmont 46k	7	2	1^{3}	1^{4}	1^{3}	1^{3}	Kurtsinger C	126	w	*.90	101-06	War Admiral126^{3}Sceneshifter126^{10}Vamoose126^{2}	Easily best	7
15May37-6Pim	gd	$1\frac{3}{16}$	$:47$ $1:12^{2}$ $1:37^{3}$ $1:58^{2}$		Preakness 55k	1	2	1^{1}	1^{1}	1^{hd}	1^{hd}	Kurtsinger C	126	w	*.35	98-16	War Admiral126^{hd}Pompoon126^{8}Flying Scot126^{2}	Hard drive	8
8May37-6CD	fst	1¼	$:46^{4}$ $1:12^{2}$ $1:37^{2}$ $2:03^{1}$		Ky Derby 62k	1	2	$1^{1\frac{1}{2}}$	$1^{1\frac{1}{2}}$	1^{3}	$1^{1\frac{3}{4}}$	Kurtsinger C	126	w	*1.60	93-11	War Admiral$126^{1\frac{3}{4}}$Pompoon126^{8}Reaping Reward126^{3}	In hand	20
24Apr37-5HdG	fst	$1\frac{1}{16}$	$:23^{2}$ $:47^{2}$ $1:11^{3}$ $1:45$		Chesapeake 11k	3	1	1^{1}	1^{2}	1^{4}	1^{6}	Kurtsinger C	119	w	*.65e	93-15	WarAdmiral119^{6}CourtScandal$119^{\frac{1}{2}}$OverthTop114^{2}	Easily best	7
14Apr37-4HdG	fst	6f	$:23$ $:46^{1}$ $1:11^{2}$		Alw 1000	2	1	1^{hd}	1^{2}	1^{3}	$1^{2\frac{1}{2}}$	Kurtsinger C	120	w	*.75	96-16	War Admiral$120^{2\frac{1}{2}}$Clingendaal111^{6}Airflame117^{3}	In hand	6
10Oct36-5Lrl	my	6f	$:23^{2}$ $:47^{3}$ $1:12^{3}$		Richard Johnson H 5k	2	2	1^{hd}	$2^{\frac{1}{2}}$	2^{2}	$2^{1\frac{1}{2}}$	Kurtsinger C	124	w	*.80	89-23	BottleCap$119^{1\frac{1}{2}}$WarAdmiral124^{8}YellowTulp$114^{1\frac{1}{2}}$	Closed well	10
19Sep36-5HdG	fst	6f	$:22^{3}$ $:45^{4}$ $1:11$		Eastern Shore H 14k	15	1	$1^{1\frac{1}{2}}$	1^{4}	1^{4}	1^{5}	Kurtsinger C	118	w	7.85	98-12	War Admiral118^{5}Orientalist116^{hd}Rex Flag115^{hd}	Easily	15
1Jly36-5Aqu	fst	6f	$:23^{2}$ $:47^{3}$ $1:12^{3}$		Great American 5.4k	6	3	1^{hd}	1^{hd}	1^{hd}	$2^{1\frac{1}{2}}$	Kurtsinger C	115	w	2.00	89-15	Fairy Hill$113^{1\frac{1}{2}}$War Admiral115^{2}Maedic$115^{\frac{1}{2}}$	Weakened	8
6Jun36-4Bel	fst	5f-WC	$:59$		National Stallion 16k	6	2		$5^{3\frac{1}{2}}$	$3^{1\frac{1}{2}}$	$3^{2\frac{1}{2}}$	Westrope J	122	w	3.00	82-14	Pompoon$122^{1\frac{1}{2}}$Fencing122^{1}War Admiral122^{hd}	Closed gamely	10
21May36-3Bel	fst	5f-WC	$:58^{4}$		©Alw 900	6	3		1^{hd}	1^{1}	1^{2}	Westrope J	113	w	10.00	86-18	War Admiral113^{2}Scintillator113^{5}Papenie116^{1}	Going away	8
25Apr36-1HdG	fst	4½f	$:23^{3}$ $:48^{3}$ $:55^{1}$		Md Sp Wt	9	4		2^{hd}	$2^{\frac{1}{2}}$	1no	Peters M	114	w	7.50	89-11	War Admiral114^{no}Sonny Joe114^{1}Ground Oak$114^{2\frac{1}{2}}$	Hard drive	10

Index

Photo Credits

Page 1: War Admiral (The Blood-Horse); War Admiral head shot (Morgan Photo Service)

Page 2: Fair Play (The Blood-Horse); Man o' War (Keeneland-McClure); Sweep (The Blood-Horse); Brushup (The Blood-Horse)

Page 3: Samuel D. Riddle (Morgan Photo Service); George Conway and George Cassidy (C.C. Cook); Charley Kurtsinger aboard War Admiral (The Blood-Horse)

Page 4: Conway watching his horses (Joe Fleischer); After winning the Chesapeake (Morgan Photo Service)

Page 5: Winning the Kentucky Derby; in the Derby winner's circle (both The Blood-Horse); Winning the Preakness (Morgan Photo Service)

Page 6: Winning the Belmont (NYRA); Returning to winner's circle (Morgan Photo Service); Belmont trophy presentation (Keeneland-Morgan)

Page 7: War Admiral with Mrs. Riddle and Conway (Morgan Photo Service); Winning the Washington Handicap (Turf Pix); Winning the Heather Purse (The Blood-Horse)

Page 8: In the Widener Cup (Keeneland-Morgan); Training at Hialeah (C.C. Cook); At Hialeah with Conway (C.C. Cook)

Page 9: Winning the Saratoga Handicap (Keeneland-Morgan); Winning the Whitney and the Saratoga Cup (both Keeneland-Cook)

Page 10: Winning the Jockey Club Gold Cup (Keeneland-Morgan); Gold Cup winner's circle (Keeneland-Cook)

Page 11: C.S. Howard and Riddle (Joe Fleischer); War Admiral with Riddle (Joe Fleischer); War Admiral acting up (Int'l News Photograph Service)

Page 12: Seabiscuit and War Admiral each work for match race (both Joe Fleischer)

Page 13: Pimlico Special "match race" post parade; Seabiscuit wins match race (both Joe Fleischer)

Page 14: War Admiral arrives in Lexington (The Blood-Horse); War Admiral with Will Harbut (Jack Wilkes/LIFE Magazine)

Page 15: Searching (Bert and Richard Morgan); Busher (Bert Morgan); Blue Peter (Marshall Hawkins); Busanda (Bert Morgan)

Page 16: War Admiral at Hamburg Place (Warren Schraeder); Gravestone (Lucy Zeh)

E dward L. Bowen is the author of more than twenty books on Thoroughbred racing history. He was a staff member of the weekly trade publication *The Blood-Horse* for some thirty years, including seventeen as managing editor and five as editor-in-chief. He was also editor of *The Canadian Horse* for two years. Bowen served as president of the Grayson-Jockey Club Research Foundation from 1994 through 2018. Bowen has received various honors within the world of Thoroughbred and sports journalism and author-ship, including an Eclipse Award for magazine writing, the Charles W. Engelhard Award from the Kentucky Thoroughbred Association, the Old Hilltop Award from Pimlico Race Course, the Walter Haight Award from the National Turf Writers Association, and the gold medal designation in *Foreword*'s sports category. He resides in Versailles, Kentucky.